"We know that you can't just talk about obs
(OCD)—if you want improvement, you have
put wisdom, energy, and life in their book, as they join with youth to build
coping skills via activities that are developmentally appropriate in tone,
style, and language. OCD is treatable, and this workbook is helpful for youth
to understand OCD and for therapists to accompany therapy. The exercises
come with both readable examples and advice for how to 'stay strong'
when it gets tough. Puliafico and Robin are a team of experts bringing their
expertise to life in this readable and helpful book."

—**Philip C. Kendall, PhD, ABPP,** Distinguished University Professor
and Laura H. Carnell Professor of Psychology at Temple University

"Puliafico and Robin have done a great service for children with OCD
and their parents. The activities in the workbook are clear, structured, and
guided by the research on childhood OCD conceptualization and treatment.
As a guide to accompany treatment with a trained clinician, the exercises
here will undoubtedly serve as a great way to facilitate treatment and
provide children with relief. I recommend it enthusiastically to parents of
children with OCD and providers who regularly treat this condition."

—**Dean McKay, PhD, ABPP,** professor of psychology at
Fordham University

"In *The OCD Workbook for Kids*, Puliafico and Robin have created a
masterpiece in the form of a step-by-step approach for helping children
struggling with OCD (and their parents) in understanding and addressing
this impairing condition. The writing style is fun, clear, and kid/parent
friendly, and the text describes the core treatment components in an easy-
to-understand manner. Given the difficulty that so many families of a child
with OCD experience in accessing effective care, this book has the promise
to help many children live their fullest, happiest life."

—**Eric Storch, PhD,** professor and All Children's Hospital Guild
Endowed Chair at the University of South Florida

"As a child and adolescent psychiatrist that works with children diagnosed with OCD and their families, this workbook provides a much-needed resource for not only children and families living with OCD, but also for providers. The authors present the material in a way that is both understandable and engaging for young readers, and the many examples, activities, and handouts provide ample guidance for children, parents, and therapists."

> —**Moira A. Rynn, MD**, consulting professor and chair in the department of psychiatry and behavioral sciences at Duke University Medical Center

Publisher's Note

Distributed in Canada by Raincoast Books

Copyright © 2017 by Anthony C. Puliafico and Joanna A. Robin
        Instant Help Books
        An imprint of New Harbinger Publications, Inc.
        5674 Shattuck Avenue
        Oakland, CA 94609
        www.newharbinger.com

Cover model is used for illustrative purposes only

Cover design by Amy Shoup

Acquired by Jess O'Brien

Edited by Brady Kahn

All Rights Reserved

FSC
www.fsc.org
MIX
Paper from
responsible sources
FSC® C011935

Library of Congress Cataloging-in-Publication Data on file

19   18   17

10   9   8   7   6   5   4   3   2   1   First Printing

Contents

Part 4: Brave Challenges

Part 5: Staying Strong

Foreword

The buzzing of the intercom seemed simultaneous with the commotion in the waiting area, which could be heard throughout the clinic: "Dr. Albano, your new patient is here. Please hurry." In the waiting room, I came upon a little girl who was filled with grit and energy, and in the throes of extreme distress. "Let me go! I need to count. I need to count and touch the door. Let go!" she cried, and wailed and struggled against her father, who had her in a bear hug as she kicked and scratched at him. The child's mother stood to the side in tears.

This was my first encounter with a child who was suffering with obsessive-compulsive disorder (OCD), and I was terrified. And, it was my first week as a new psychologist. Not much was understood in those days about the disorder and its impact, and even less was known about how to effectively help these children and their parents. But groundbreaking work by my colleagues John March and Edna Foa was in progress, and soon we were helping this young girl to give her OCD a nasty nickname and to engage in exposure and ritual prevention (EX/RP). Fortunately, my patient found herself in one of the centers also at the forefront of this work. An explosion of research focused on developing evidence-based treatments was happening across the country, with the Pediatric Obsessive-Compulsive Disorder Treatment Study team finding that cognitive-behavioral treatment involving EX/RP, presented in a developmentally sensitive manner, was effective in treating youth with OCD (POTS 2004) and, when delivered with expert supervision, could outperform medication treatment (Freeman et al. 2014).

Fast-forward, and Anthony Puliafico (Tony, to me) and Joanna Robin join my team as new psychologists, having received their graduate training under the direction of Dr. Philip C. Kendall, the pioneer of evidence-based treatments for child and adolescent anxiety and OCD. I had the privilege to observe and supervise their work toward licensure as clinical psychologists, and shared their delight in watching kids recover from OCD and embrace the joys of their age and stage.

Most exciting for me was seeing the ways that Drs. Puliafico and Robin breathed life into the strategies and procedures of treatment for OCD, for children and families, and the tools they developed to transfer the learning from the therapy office to the environments where children lived and played.

Parents often arrive asking, "But what can we do? Please give me something!" Children relate best to the process of therapy when it's presented through play and active exercises that engage their interests, reinforce their abilities, and increase their motivation. This workbook is the culmination of the tools developed by Drs. Puliafico and Robin in a step-by-step guide for kids and parents. Through these pages, families will learn about OCD and kids, and parents will build coping skills and the emotional fortitude to overcome this too-often devastating disorder. Drs. Puliafico and Robin help kids to focus and highlight their unique strengths, and then, through systematic exercises illustrated with clear and relatable examples, teach kids to overcome their OCD using the most well-established methods developed in clinical studies. From distinguishing regular thoughts from sticky thoughts to engaging in brave challenges that tackle symptoms and distress, these authors give kids and parents the hope, insight, and skills they need to overcome OCD. Going further, Drs. Puliafico and Robin provide specific guidance for when the going gets rough, such as when OCD interferes with school or when a child feels unmotivated or down, and spell out concise and practical strategies for parents to use in assisting their child throughout the process of therapy. Most importantly, Drs. Puliafico and Robin make it very okay for children to seek help with their OCD "team" to work their way up the brave-challenge tower to success.

This comprehensive workbook is appropriate for school-aged children and closely involves their parents or supervising adults in the process. Therapists who are working with children will find this workbook a true pleasure to accompany therapy, as every resource for treating OCD is in one place ready for use. Thank you, Drs. Puliafico and Robin, for this welcome resource!

—Anne Marie Albano, PhD, ABPP
Professor of Medical Psychology in Psychiatry
   at Columbia University Medical Center
Director, Columbia University Clinic for Anxiety
   and Related Disorders

A Letter to Caregivers

Dear Caregiver,

If you are reading this, chances are you have a child who struggles with obsessive-compulsive disorder, or OCD. OCD is a disorder that affects approximately one in fifty individuals (Ruscio, Stein, Chiu, and Kessler 2010). When a child suffers from OCD, it can often affect a whole family. As a caregiver, it may be hard to know how to respond when you notice your child feeling very distressed, avoiding important situations, or caught in a loop of doing the same behavior over and over. Our hope is that this workbook can guide both you and your child in dealing with your child's OCD more effectively.

Oftentimes OCD can go unnoticed by parents and caregivers either because they do not know the warning signs or because their children try their best to hide their symptoms. By recognizing that your child is struggling with OCD, you have taken an important step in helping your child!

The good news is that OCD is highly treatable. In fact, the principles that form the foundation of this workbook are based on exposure and ritual prevention (EX/RP) therapy, which is the frontline therapy for children with OCD. This book is intended to help kids and families better manage OCD symptoms and may be used either as a first step for families learning about OCD or as a supplement to treatment. We encourage you to preview the content of this book before reading it with your child. Because OCD sometimes focuses on sensitive topics, make sure that the content in each activity is appropriate for *your* child.

Whereas this book can be used effectively as a supplement to EX/RP therapy, it is not a substitute for therapy. If your child's OCD is significantly interfering with his or her functioning at home, at school, or socially, seeking treatment with a professional may be appropriate.

Our sincere hope is that this workbook will help your child understand OCD and respond to OCD symptoms more effectively. There is also a host of materials, including PDFs of many of the worksheets, available for download at the website for this book: http://www.newharbinger.com/39782. (See the very back of this book for more details.)

Best regards,

Tony Puliafico and Joanna Robin

Part 1

Getting to Know Your OCD

What Exactly is OCD?

For You to Know

You are probably reading this book because you are dealing with something called OCD. The point of this book is to teach kids all about OCD and what they can do about it. By starting to read this book, you just took a big first step toward beating your OCD!

We want you to get three big things out of reading this book:

1. We want you to learn a lot about OCD, so you know exactly when it bothers you.

2. We want you to read about lots of other kids who are dealing with OCD, so you know how other kids handle it.

3. We want to help you practice some ways to stand up to OCD so that you can be your best at home, at school, and with your friends.

Overall, we want this book to help you become stronger than OCD!

Here are the basic facts about OCD:

OCD stands for **Obsessive Compulsive Disorder**

There are two parts to OCD: **Obsessions** and **Compulsions**.

OCD is Common!

One in every 200 people in the U.S. suffer from OCD. That means there are probably other people with OCD on your block or in your school!

OCD is Treatable!

There are things you and your family can do to help beat your OCD.

OCD is Not Your Fault!

You didn't do anything wrong to cause your OCD.

OCD is considered a medical problem, just like asthma.

There is one other important thing to know: OCD works like a trap. It makes you feel bad, and then it tricks you into thinking that the only way to feel better is to follow its rules. These rules can be really specific, and they may involve washing your hands a lot, checking over and over to make sure bad things will not happen, or repeating the same thing many times until it feels "right."

This is what OCD wants you to think:

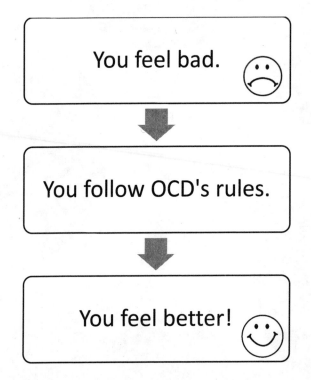

When you follow OCD's rules, you do feel better—for a few minutes maybe. But then, soon enough, that bad feeling comes right back. This is usually what *really* happens:

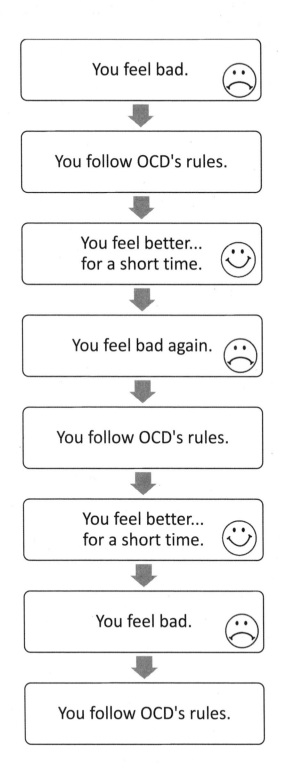

And this cycle can go on and on and on. Does this sound familiar to you? Do you feel trapped by your OCD?

This book is meant to help you get out of the OCD trap. But before talking more about OCD, we want to focus on you. Because there is *much* more to you than just OCD.

For You to Do

Kids sometimes forget about all of the great parts of their lives when they are living with OCD. With the help of this book, you can become stronger than OCD. That way, you can make sure that OCD doesn't bother all of the other great parts of your life.

Fill in this portrait of yourself with words and pictures:

Favorite Hobbies	Things I Am Proud Of

A Picture of Me

Favorite Subjects in School	People That Make Me Happy

Great job! There are so many important parts of your life. Getting stronger than OCD will help you enjoy them even more!

More for You to Do

Getting stronger than OCD can be hard work sometimes. Many kids find it helpful to remember the reasons they want to get stronger than OCD.

In the space provided, write down three reasons you want to get stronger than OCD. First look at the reasons that a girl named Beth gave for getting stronger than OCD. You can use Beth's reasons as a guide:

1. **My OCD rules made my bedtime routine very long and annoying.**

2. **I wanted to spend time with my friends without having to follow OCD's rules.**

3. **OCD made it hard for me to pay attention in class.**

Now it's your turn.

I want to get stronger than OCD because…

1. _____

2. _____

3. _____

Sometimes, getting stronger than OCD can be hard. If you ever start finding it very hard to do the activities in this book, come back to this page and remember all the great reasons why you want to get stronger than OCD!

Activity 2

Regular Thoughts Vs. Sticky Thoughts

For You to Know

Did you ever get a song stuck in your head and you wished you could stop humming or singing it? This can be so annoying! But it's very normal and happens to most kids and grown-ups. When you have OCD, your thoughts are much stickier and it's harder to get these thoughts out of your head. Lots of times, these thoughts make kids feel uncomfortable or nervous that something bad will happen or that something is wrong with them. The fancy name for these thoughts and images is *obsessions*, but we call them *sticky thoughts*. Remember how we talked about OCD being like a trap? Well, many kids fall into that trap because they want to get rid of their sticky thoughts as quickly as possible!

So, how do you tell the difference between a regular thought and a sticky thought? Here are some tips for how to tell them apart.

Regular Thoughts...	*Sticky Thoughts...*
Come and go quickly.	Stay around for long periods of time.
Might make you feel scared or concerned, but you can make yourself feel better easily.	Can make you feel very scared or grossed out, and you cannot make yourself feel better easily.
Rarely return if you don't want them to.	Keep coming back.
Can be about anything.	Are usually about things you don't like to think about.
Usually come and go on their own, so you don't feel like you need to do anything to make the thoughts go away.	May make you feel like you need to do something over and over again to make the thoughts go away.

You are on your way to understanding the difference between regular thoughts and sticky thoughts!

For You to Do

It can sometimes be difficult to figure out the difference between regular thoughts and sticky thoughts. It helps to practice.

A list of thoughts follows. Put an *R* next to thoughts that you think are *regular thoughts* and an *S* next to thoughts that may be *sticky thoughts*.

Thoughts	*Regular (R) or Sticky (S)*
Kyle wonders what he is having for dinner tonight and then completes his homework.	
Bella thinks, *There might be a fire in my house*, during class, and has trouble focusing on what her teacher is saying.	
Chris worries, *I might get sick if I touch doorknobs*, so he avoids opening doors on his own.	
Beth hopes she gets to hang out with her friends tonight.	
Maggie imagines hurting her dog, even though she loves him and wouldn't want anything bad to happen to him.	

Answer Key: *R, S, S, R, S*

Check over your answers using the answer key and see how you did. Great job! Now you know the difference between sticky thoughts and regular thoughts!

More for You to Do

Sometimes parents and teachers tell you to just not think about stressful or scary things, but that usually doesn't work so well. Actually, when you try to stop thinking about something, it usually sticks around more!

As an experiment, try this. When we say "Go!" close your eyes and try your very hardest to *not* think about a polka-dotted penguin. Try really hard to *not* think about this silly polka-dotted penguin with rainbow colors all over it! Ready...set... close your eyes...Go!

Okay, how did that go? If you are like most people, telling yourself not to think about something actually makes you think about it more. When you have sticky thoughts or images in your head, trying hard not to think about them makes them stick around even longer. Or they might go away for a little bit but come back a few minutes later. That can be very difficult! But don't worry—this book will help you learn new ways to handle your sticky thoughts and feel better!

For You to Know

Sticky thoughts are one part of OCD. They are those thoughts or images (pictures in your head) that you don't like to have. Like we said in activity 2, we like to call them sticky thoughts because they stick around your head and can be scary or annoying. Lots of times they make kids feel uncomfortable or nervous that something bad will happen or that something is wrong with them.

Let's read about Terrell's sticky thoughts:

Terrell found it very hard to pay attention in class. Whenever he was in class, he had sticky thoughts that he might become like other kids in the class if he touched them or their stuff. He was especially worried that he would become less smart if he touched kids who he thought were not as smart as he was. Terrell felt the need to watch where these kids sat and what they touched in his classroom so that he could avoid touching anything they touched. Terrell knew his sticky thoughts made no sense and that he could not really become less smart by touching another kid. But his sticky thoughts were so scary that he almost always listened to them.

Here are some more examples of sticky thoughts that kids may have:

My parents might have left the stove on and the house might burn down.

I might get sick from touching that bathroom faucet.

Sometimes sticky thoughts feel more like a bad or *not-right* feeling that you don't like. These feelings may seem silly to others, but to you it's just the way you feel.

Here's an example:

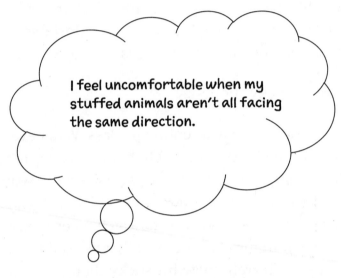

> I feel uncomfortable when my stuffed animals aren't all facing the same direction.

For some kids, sticky thoughts are more like images or pictures in their heads that they don't like. These images are usually about doing or saying things that you never would actually want to do. Here's an example:

> I imagine tripping kids in the school hallway, and I don't want to do it! But what if I really do want to do it?

Sticky thoughts can be scary! What helps lots of kids is to remember that sticky thoughts are really *just thoughts*, and having them doesn't mean bad things will happen or that you are a bad person. In other words, *sticky thoughts don't matter.* We have silly thoughts all the time, and most of them are not true. In fact, you can practice having a silly thought. Think to yourself, *I will turn into a cheeseburger.* Think really hard about becoming that cheeseburger…

Well, did you turn into a cheeseburger? Most sticky thoughts are just as silly as thoughts about becoming a cheeseburger!

For You to Do

Sticky thoughts can be about all types of things, but here are some common sticky thoughts that kids have.

Sticky Thoughts Checklist

Place a check mark next to the ones that sound like you.

- ☐ *I might have germs on me.*

- ☐ *I feel dirty or disgusting.*

- ☐ *Something bad might happen to me or to someone I love.*

- ☐ *I might not remember information I need to know later.*

- ☐ *I feel like my work needs to be perfect.*

- ☐ *I might throw away something I need later.*

- ☐ *I am afraid I made God angry.*

- ☐ *I am afraid I made my family or friends angry.*

- ☐ *I have images in my head that are very upsetting.*

- ☐ *I feel uncomfortable if I don't arrange things in a certain way.*

- ☐ *I just feel "not right" if I don't follow OCD's rules.*

Some kids have just one or two sticky thoughts that bother them, and other kids have a whole lot. Whether you have lots of sticky thoughts or just a few, this book will help teach you how to handle them!

More for You to Do

Now try to write down the sticky thoughts that you have like the ones on the previous page. Here's one of Terrell's sticky thoughts as an example:

If I touch that kid, I will become less smart.

Use the checklist to remember the sticky thoughts that bother you a lot, and write them down inside the thought bubbles.

Understanding Your Sticky Thoughts

Sticky Thoughts That Bother You a Lot

Great job writing down your sticky thoughts! It will be helpful to keep these in mind as you read the rest of this book. Now that you know the sticky thoughts that bother you, you're one step closer to getting stronger than OCD!

For You to Know

You just learned about one big part of OCD: those annoying sticky thoughts. The *other* big part of OCD is following all of the rules that OCD tells you to follow. Kids often have to follow OCD rules over and over again. These things you do over and over to follow OCD's rules are called *compulsions*. To help learn more about compulsions, here is a story about Lily and her compulsions:

> Lily worried a lot about something bad happening to her family members. She liked to feel certain that she did everything she could to keep them safe. Lily checked the door in her apartment many times before going to bed to make sure it was locked so that a stranger would not come in. She also checked the oven many times to make sure it was turned off. Sometimes, Lily's checking prevented her from finishing her homework on time or watching her favorite TV show. Lily's parents would often say, "You just checked! Why do you need to check again?" Lily knew it was silly to check the doors and oven over and over again, but when she had a thought about something bad happening, checking was the only thing that made her feel better.

Doing compulsions can get very annoying and take up lots of time. Do you want to know something else about compulsions? They do not work! Think about it—if doing compulsions worked, why would you have to do them over and over and over again?!?

We'll tell you more in the next activity about why doing compulsions doesn't work. This next exercise will help you figure out what your compulsions are.

For You to Do

Compulsions can be about all kinds of things. This is a list of some common ones.

Common Compulsions Checklist

Place a check mark next to the ones that sound like you.

☐ *I wash my hands, shower, or clean my stuff a lot.*

☐ *I check to make sure things are safe.*

☐ *I ask my parents a lot of questions to make sure we are safe.*

☐ *I read things over and over.*

☐ *I write things over and over until they look perfect.*

☐ *I save stuff that I may need later even if other people think it's garbage.*

☐ *I repeat my prayers over and over or say prayers a lot.*

☐ *I check in with people a lot to make sure they are not angry with me.*

☐ *I think a lot about how I acted to make sure I did not do something wrong.*

☐ *I need to keep my things arranged in a certain way.*

☐ *I repeat some things I do until it feels "right."*

☐ *I ask my parents the same questions over and over.*

☐ *I think or say "good" words or phrases to cancel out "bad" words or phrases.*

More for You to Do

Lily became annoyed when she checked the doors and oven in her apartment. She wished she didn't have to, but she felt very upset if she tried not to. Do you find your compulsions annoying but you do them anyway?

Looking back at the checklist, write down the compulsions that bother you the most.

Compulsions That Bother You

1. _____

2. _____

3. _____

4. _____

5. _____

Excellent work! Now you know your sticky thoughts *and* the compulsions that you do when you have those sticky thoughts. Learning lots about your OCD is the best way to start outsmarting it!

Why OCD's Rules Don't Work!

For You to Know

Can you think of any rules that just don't work for you? Maybe your parents have a rule that you need to wear nice clothes to a restaurant, but you only like to wear a T-shirt and jeans. Maybe you have to make your bed every morning even though you know you will just mess up your bed again at night!

Well, OCD makes up some pretty bad rules too. Most of the time, OCD's rules involve doing compulsions, but sometimes OCD's rules involve avoiding certain places or people. Here is a story about Jimmy and one of his OCD rules:

> When Jimmy is at church with his family, he has upsetting sticky thoughts about saying curse words to God. Jimmy doesn't want to do this, but his sticky thoughts say, *Maybe you do really want to curse at God. Maybe that's why you're thinking about it!* Jimmy's OCD rule is that he has to say ten prayers whenever he has the sticky thought about cursing at God. The problem is that as soon as Jimmy finishes these prayers, he has another sticky thought and has to do his praying all over again. On most days, Jimmy ends up doing his praying compulsions for the entire church service. Jimmy is usually exhausted by the end of church and realizes that he did not pay attention to anything besides his sticky thoughts and compulsions.

Does Jimmy's story sound familiar? You may have noticed that your compulsions are taking up more time than they used to. You may have also noticed that OCD has created new rules or that you have to follow more rules now than you used to. If you're like other kids with OCD, you may follow OCD's rules because you are afraid your sticky thoughts will never go away unless you do. But actually, what we know about OCD is that your sticky thoughts eventually stop bothering you *even if you do not follow OCD's rules.* In fact, the more you just let your sticky thoughts come and go on their own, the more you will learn that you can handle them and that bad things won't happen just because your sticky thoughts say they will!

It's time to come up with a new game plan, because you don't want to follow OCD's rules any longer!

New Game Plan

1. Allow yourself to have sticky thoughts whenever they come up. They are only thoughts, and *they do not matter*!

2. Say no to following OCD's rules and doing compulsions when you have sticky thoughts.

Now, this plan may sound a bit hard right now. That's why we will be teaching you different skills to help you get stronger than OCD. There is no need to try breaking all of OCD's rules just yet—it can be very difficult to start breaking every rule all at once. For now, just keep reading and learning more about OCD, and we'll let you know when it's rule-breaking time!

Why OCD's Rules Don't Work!

For You to Do

Think about the rules that OCD tells you to follow. Your rules may be to do the compulsions you listed in activity 4 or to avoid certain places or people. It's time to figure out if these rules work for you.

Here is an example from Jimmy:

Jimmy's OCD Rule	
Rule	*Is It Good for You?*
I need to say ten prayers every time I have a sticky thought about cursing at God.	No. It is very annoying, and I don't pay attention at church.

Now list some of your OCD rules and decide if these rules are good for you or not:

Your OCD Rules	
Rule	*Is It Good for You?*
1.	
2.	
3.	

Review your list. Do your OCD rules take up a lot of time or get in the way of doing things you enjoy? Do your OCD rules really work for *you*?

OCD Workbook for Kids

More for You to Do

Jimmy started calling OCD the "Time Monster" because it took up a lot of his free time.

What are some reasons why OCD's rules don't work for you? Write these reasons down or draw about them in the space provided.

Why OCD's Rules Don't Work

1. _____

2. _____

3. _____

4. _____

Keep these reasons in mind as you read this book. They'll help motivate you to keep getting stronger than OCD!

Part 2

You and Your OCD

How Does OCD Affect Your life?

For You to Know

OCD can affect kids differently. For some kids, OCD interferes with most of their day, including school, hobbies, relationships, and even sleep. For other kids, OCD pops up during specific situations, like only at bedtime or when they are in the bathroom. These kids only notice OCD interfering at these times. It is important to figure out the ways that OCD messes up things in your life so that you can make a plan to help you become stronger than OCD. Here is a story about Aliza and how she noticed OCD interfering with different parts of her life.

Aliza was really getting frustrated with her OCD. While she was at school, she kept having sticky thoughts that she may have cheated on her quizzes and tests. She wanted these sticky thoughts to go away. She kept telling herself that she didn't cheat, but the thoughts that she was cheating kept coming back. Her sticky thoughts became so bothersome that she confessed to her teacher that she had cheated! Aliza's teacher reassured her that she had watched the whole class take the test and didn't think she had cheated. This made Aliza feel a little better, but the next day her sticky thoughts about cheating came back again!

Aliza noticed that OCD was interfering with her schoolwork. She wrote down two ways that OCD was messing things up at school for her. This is what she wrote:

1. I cannot focus on learning, because of my sticky thoughts.

2. I keep interrupting the lesson to confess to the teacher.

OCD also started to bother Aliza at nighttime. When she got into bed, sticky thoughts about cheating would pop into her head and, just like at school, she felt that she needed to confess. When this happened, Aliza would run into her parents' room to confess that she might have cheated on a test. Her parents always tried to reassure her, but she still needed to check with them three or four times each night. In the morning, Aliza would be really tired! This made it hard to focus, and it made her kind of grouchy too.

Aliza's OCD was affecting her sleep, making it hard for her to get through the day because she was so tired, and affecting her relationships with her family. She wrote down the ways OCD was affecting her sleep. This is what she wrote:

1. **I am wasting time following OCD's rules to confess when I should be sleeping!**

2. **When I spend time confessing instead of sleeping, I notice that I am grouchy the next day, and I am not kind to my sister or my parents.**

Interfering with school and with sleep are two examples of how OCD can affect the lives of kids. Some kids notice that OCD affects them when they eat, when they go to the bathroom, when they play sports, when they read, and in many other situations.

For You to Do

Take a moment to think of the different ways that OCD affects your life.

In the table, describe how OCD has messed things up for you in these different areas.

Life Areas	Does OCD mess up this area? If so, how does OCD mess things up?
School	
Friendships	
Family	
Sleep	
Eating Healthy	
How You Feel	
Hobbies	
Other: _____	

OCD Workbook for Kids

More for You to Do

It can be overwhelming to have these different areas of your life affected by OCD, but we want you to stay focused on your goal to become stronger than OCD. One way to do this is visualize what you want your life to look like without OCD messing things up.

Take a moment to close your eyes and imagine yourself not following OCD's rules. This can happen if you stay focused on your goal. In the space below, write or draw about how your life would be different if OCD were not messing things up for you.

You did a great job of figuring out how OCD affects your life and what you want your life to look like in the future. You are on your way to becoming stronger than OCD!

What Is Your OCD's Name?

For You to Know

When you have OCD, you end up doing a lot of compulsions that you wish you didn't have to do. You probably would rather be playing or hanging out with friends instead of listening to OCD's rules. Sometimes it might feel like your whole life is about dealing with OCD! Learning how to see OCD as *a problem you have* and not part of you can help you become stronger than OCD!

One way to do this is to come up with a name for OCD. A doctor named John March suggested that giving OCD a name helps kids see OCD as the problem rather than see themselves or their parents as the problem (March and Mulle 1998). It's a good idea for you to try to come up with a silly name or names that put down OCD, because we want you to remember that you are stronger than OCD.

One boy named Matthew gave OCD a few different names to help him become stronger than his OCD.

One of Matthew's OCD rules was related to checking. Before he left for school, he always checked to make sure he turned off his light, turned off the water in the bathroom, and closed the refrigerator door. Matthew checked several times, and if interrupted, he had to start the checking all over again. It was difficult for him to get to school on time because he was so busy checking.

Matthew's parents were upset because they were often late for work due to his checking. Matthew started to feel like a big problem for his family until his parents told him that he wasn't the problem—OCD was. They told Matthew that it would be helpful to come up with a name for OCD, so they could easily talk about it without making Matthew feel bad. Matthew wanted to come up with a silly name, so he came up with the name Checky. He thought that he wouldn't want to listen to someone named Checky. When Checky would show up, Matthew would say, "Checky is so pushy this morning. He keeps telling me to check to make sure I turned off the light, but I know I turned it off." Instead of feeling mad at himself, Matthew was mad at Checky. This made him want to say no to Checky. Using the name Checky also helped his parents. They would say to Matthew, "Let's tell Checky to take a rocket ship to outer space and never come back."

For You to Do

Come up with a name for your OCD. Matthew came up with Checky, but there are lots of names he could have used. Below are some other names kids have called OCD:

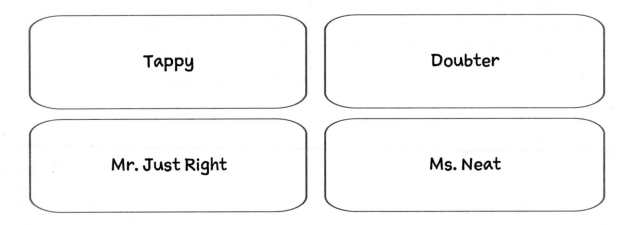

Tappy

Doubter

Mr. Just Right

Ms. Neat

You can name OCD anything you want, but we ask that you try to name it something that will make you feel stronger than OCD. In the space below, write down the name that you would like to call OCD:

I will call my OCD _____

More for You to Do

It can also be helpful to visualize OCD as a silly character.

Fill in the blank with OCD's new name, and then draw a picture of what OCD looks like in the box.

Here is what _____ *looks like:*

. . . .
.   .
.   .
.   .
.   .
.   .
.   .
.   .
.   .
.   .
.   .
.   .
.   .
.   .
.   .
.   .
.   .
.   .
.   .
.   .
.   .
. . . .

Now that you have a name for OCD, you and your parents can practice talking about it using this name. Talking about OCD as something separate from you will help you feel stronger than OCD!

Who's on Your Team?

For You to Know

When you have OCD, you may feel lonely or that no one really understands how hard it can be to have OCD. But if you are like most kids with OCD, your family members and friends can help! We have found that a great way to cope with OCD is to build a team of people you trust to help you stand up to OCD.

Alex and Michael are two boys who cope with OCD in different ways.

> Alex had always been a really independent kid. He enjoyed figuring out difficult math problems on his own and searching on the Internet for answers to questions that he didn't understand. So when Alex started to have sticky thoughts, he assumed that this too was a problem he could solve on his own. He couldn't understand why he suddenly was afraid to touch things others had touched. Alex knew that something was wrong, but he thought he should be able to handle it without his parents' help. When his parents asked him why he seemed nervous, he did not tell them about his sticky thoughts, because he didn't want to admit that he needed help. Alex started to feel very sad, because he did not know how to handle OCD.

> Michael started having sticky thoughts about something bad happening to his dog when he was not at home. He started checking the door five times and hugging his dog ten times every time he left the house. Even though Michael was embarrassed, he explained to his parents why he was following all of these rules. He felt so much better afterward! Michael and his parents did some research and found out that Michael had OCD. His parents told him that they would help him overcome OCD and that working as a team could be a good approach.

Alex and Michael both struggled with OCD on their own for a little while, but when Michael was able to talk to his parents about his sticky thoughts and OCD rules, he didn't feel so alone and scared. He also felt better knowing that his parents would be part of his team.

Accepting help from others can be difficult for many different reasons. Michael felt a little embarrassed at first when he asked for help, and Alex felt like he *shouldn't need* help. The good news is that Alex eventually realized that he needed help dealing with OCD and then spoke to his parents about it. He was glad that he did, because they were able to help him come up with a plan to work as a team.

You can benefit from having a team, just like Alex and Michael have. Here are some things a team member can do:

- Listen to you when you are struggling with OCD

- Help you notice sticky thoughts and OCD's rules

- Encourage you to become stronger than OCD and not give in to compulsions

- Help set up brave challenges with you (you'll learn about brave challenges soon!)

For You to Do

Think about family members, therapists, or teachers that you could ask to be on your team. These should be people you can trust and are willing to help support you.

Here is Michael's list:

Team Members	Ways They Can Help
Mom and Dad	Helping me resist my checking by cheering me on
My teacher, Mr. Thompson	Help me focus on schoolwork instead of my dog
Ms. Green, my counselor at school	Help with ways to stand up to OCD when at school
Dr. Kerr, my therapist	Help me come up with ways to be stronger than OCD

List the members you would like to have on your team and ways that they can help:

Your Team Members	Ways They Can Help

Now make a plan with your closest team member—usually one or both parents or caretakers—about how you will tell other team members about OCD. Think about what parts of dealing with OCD you want to share with each person. Do you feel comfortable sharing the sticky thoughts and compulsions that you listed in this book? You may not feel comfortable sharing *every* part of your OCD with *every* team member, but it is important that at least one team member knows about your OCD as well as you do.

More for You to Do

Come up with a team name. It can be related to one of your favorite sports teams or a name that inspires you to be courageous.

Fill in the blank with your team name:

_____

Can you draw a picture of a team mascot to represent your team against OCD?

Wow, you have accomplished a lot in this activity. Working with your team will help you become stronger than OCD!

What's Your Rating?

For You to Know

It can sometimes be hard to explain how uncomfortable OCD is making you feel. You can use a rating scale to figure out how much OCD is bothering you. Using a rating scale can help you tell members of your team how you are feeling. An OCD rating scale is similar to a thermometer measuring the temperature outside. Just like a thermometer, which shows the red line going up when it's getting hot outside, your rating will be high when OCD is strong and you feel uncomfortable.

Here is a story about a nine-year-old girl named Sara who found using a rating scale to be very helpful.

Sara's OCD told her that she had to follow specific rules to keep others safe when she left the house. For example, one of OCD's rules was "You might have a cold, so don't touch anything in the store. You will get other people sick!" One day, Sara and her mom were in the supermarket parking lot, and Sara's OCD was so strong that she was afraid to leave the car. Sara didn't know what to do. Sara knew they needed food and that she couldn't stay in the car alone.

When Sara told her mom what was happening, her mom took out a piece of paper and drew something that looked like a number line. She labeled the number line with the numbers 0 to 10 and told her that the number 10 stood for the most uncomfortable Sara could feel; on the other end of the number line, the 0 stood for when Sara felt comfortable. She then asked Sara to use this scale of 0 to 10 to rate how uncomfortable it would be to do various tasks at the supermarket. There were a few things that were easy, others that seemed hard but doable, and a few that seemed really hard. Rating OCD helped Sara realize that she could handle certain parts of going to the supermarket, and it helped Sara's mom know how much Sara could handle at that moment. Sara and her mom made a plan to go into the supermarket, and Sara felt proud of what she was able to accomplish.

Sara used a rating scale called a *number line rating scale.*

0	1	2	3	4	5	6	7	8	9	10

Not uncomfortable at all	A little uncomfortable	Pretty uncomfortable	Very uncomfortable	Super uncomfortable	Extremely uncomfortable

Some younger kids find it easier to use a different type of rating scale called a *traffic light rating scale.*

> When Sara was younger, OCD interfered with her ability to make decisions. For example, when she would get dressed in the morning, she couldn't decide what clothes to wear, because OCD told her she would feel nervous if she made the wrong choice. Her parents introduced the traffic light rating system—red for stop, yellow for caution, and green for go—to help her rate how nervous she felt when making different decisions. Although it was still difficult for Sara to make decisions, by using the traffic light it was much easier for Sara to communicate how she was feeling, and she was able to start rating her symptoms with some help from her parents.

Just like a real traffic light, there are three possible ratings: red, yellow, and green. When you feel that OCD is easy to handle and you don't need to listen to sticky thoughts, then you rate yourself green. That means you are ready to go! When OCD is stronger and you are having difficulty standing up to OCD, you rate it a yellow, because it's slowing you down. Finally, when OCD is very strong and you feel highly uncomfortable, then you rate it a red, because you feel that OCD is stopping you.

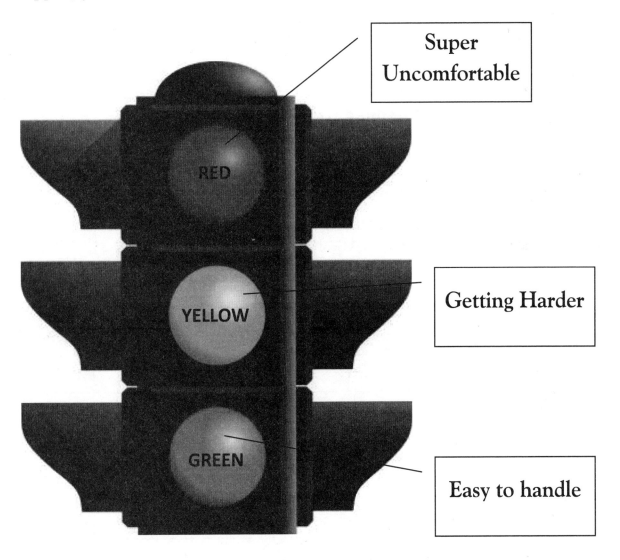

Super Uncomfortable

Getting Harder

Easy to handle

For You to Do

You can use either the number line rating scale or the traffic light rating scale to rate your situations. Here are some examples of how Sara used rating scales to help her explain how uncomfortable OCD was making her feel.

Sara's Number-Line Rating Scale

Situations at the supermarket	Rating
Touching fruit	8
Putting a few boxed or canned items in the cart	6
Pushing the cart while mom shopped	4
Walking into supermarket while mom shopped	3
Walking up to the door of the supermarket	1

Sara's Traffic-Light Rating Scale

Decision-making situations	Rating
Ordering food at a restaurant	Red
Choosing clothing to wear	Red
Using the traffic-light rating system	Yellow
Choosing something to eat for breakfast	Green
Choosing an ice cream flavor at home	Green

What's Your Rating?   Activity 9

Now it is your turn to give it a try! In the first column write down some situations that you would like to be able to do without following OCD's rules! In the second column rate how difficult these situations are for you. If you notice that they are all high ratings, try to break the situations down into smaller parts the way Sara's mom did for Sara when she was afraid to touch food at the supermarket.

Your Rating Scale

Situation	Rating

More for You to Do

Using a rating scale will help you and your team come up with ways to break down tasks and help you become stronger than OCD. Can you show a team member your rating scale and explain how you use it?

You did a great job learning about rating scales and working on your own. Later on you will be asked to use your rating scale in certain situations, so don't forget to come back to this activity if it helps.

Keeping Track of Your Compulsions

For You to Know

Imagine that your mom hid your favorite cookies and you wanted to figure out where she was hiding them. Think about how you could look for clues, just like a detective. You would probably pay *very close* attention to everything your mom did so that you could get clues about where the cookies were!

The next skill we want you to learn involves being a detective. You are going to get clues about OCD! We want you to get really good at paying attention to your compulsions: when you do them, where you do them, and how often you do them. We want you learn everything you can about your compulsions.

We also want you to keep track of what you learn—we call this *tracking*. Tracking your compulsions is easy. It just involves placing a little mark on a special tracking form every time you do a compulsion. Here's a story about how a kid named Bobby started tracking his compulsions.

> Bobby had a lot of sticky thoughts about getting sick if he touched something dirty. He worried that he might catch a disease if he was not very careful about what he touched. After a while, Bobby's OCD started really getting in the way for him at school and at his favorite hobby, swimming. Bobby started meeting with an OCD expert and learned to keep track of his compulsions so that he could know exactly when and where OCD bothered him most. Bobby decided to start tracking two compulsions that bothered him a lot. One compulsion was washing his hands whenever they felt dirty. The other compulsion was holding his breath whenever he was around people he believed were sick.

When Bobby tracked his compulsions, he placed a tally mark—which is just a straight line—on his tracking form every time he did one of these compulsions. This is what Bobby's tracking form looked like after one week:

Activity 10 Keeping Track of Your Compulsions

Day	Compulsion 1: Washing Hands	Compulsion 2: Holding Breath
Sunday	|||||||	||||
Monday	|||||||||||	|||||||||
Tuesday	||||		
Wednesday	||||||||||	|||||
Thursday	|||	|||
Friday	||||||||||||||	|||||||||||||
Saturday	|||||	||

By tracking his compulsions, Bobby noticed that he did more compulsions on Monday and Friday, which were the days when he had swimming practice and had to change in the locker room. He realized that he had to work harder to resist washing his hands and holding his breath when he had swimming practice than he did at other times.

For You to Do

Try tracking your compulsions over the next week. Start with two compulsions that bother you a lot.

Keeping Track of Your Compulsions

Write down two compulsions that you plan to track this week.

1. _____

2. _____

Now list the same two compulsions on the tracking form. Then each day of the week, pay close attention and place a tally mark every time you catch yourself doing that compulsion. If you become annoyed with tracking your compulsions, stick with it anyway. Tracking your compulsions may feel annoying at times, but it's helping you become strong enough to fight OCD!

Day	Compulsion 1: _____	Compulsion 2: _____
Sunday		
Monday		
Tuesday		
Wednesday		
Thursday		
Friday		
Saturday		

If you have kept track for one or two weeks, have you learned more about when your compulsions are hardest to resist? If you want to try keeping track of your compulsions again, you can download another copy of this tracking form at http://www.newharbinger.com/39782.

More for You to Do

Sometimes kids do compulsions without even thinking about them, which makes those compulsions hard to track! Ask a member or two of your team to tell you when they notice you doing the two compulsions that you are tracking. Your team members may notice times that you miss. With their help, you'll do an even better job of tracking your compulsions!

Which team member(s) can you ask to help you track of your compulsions?

_____

Good luck tracking!!

Part 3

Getting Stronger Than Your OCD

Standing Up to Your OCD

For You to Know

Did you ever notice that OCD can be very bossy and intimidating? When OCD is telling you to follow its rules, it can be very difficult to stand up to OCD. This activity is going to teach you things you can say to yourself to stand up to OCD's rules. We call these *stand-up statements*. A lot of kids find it helpful to say or read these statements out loud or to themselves when their OCD is trying to boss them around.

Here is an example of a girl named Jaden, who used stand-up statements to help her become stronger than OCD.

> Jaden was in third grade and had just started taking multiple-choice tests for the first time. When she sat down to take one of her first practice tests, she noticed OCD bothering her. She had a sticky thought that it didn't look right when she chose *B* two times in a row. She had another sticky thought that the letter *D* stood for "dumb" and that if she chose *D* for an answer, she would become dumb. Jaden's OCD was making her feel uncomfortable and nervous. When Jaden got home from school, she told her dad that she thought Doom-and-Gloom had bothered her during her test. She and her father called OCD "Doom-and-Gloom" because OCD always focused on bad things happening. Jaden said she knew that Doom-and-Gloom couldn't be right, but she didn't feel strong enough to just ignore her sticky thoughts. Her dad told her he was proud of her for recognizing Doom-and-Gloom and that the next step would be to come up with stand-up-statements that she could use when Doom-and-Gloom returns.

These are the stand-up statements that Jaden and her dad came up with. They wrote them down on an index card to help Jaden remember them:

> I don't have to listen to you, Doom-and-Gloom.
>
> Doom-and-Gloom, you always say that bad things are going to happen if I don't follow your rules. But you don't get to make the rules—I do.
>
> I am going to answer multiple choice questions the way I want, not the way Doom-and- Gloom wants.
>
> The teacher will let me know if I need to change my answers, not you, Doom-and-Gloom!
>
> Every time I listen to you, Doom-and-Gloom, you make things worse. So this time I am not going to listen to your rules.
>
> I can handle this uncomfortable feeling without following Doom-and-Gloom's rules!

Jaden and her teacher came up with a plan for her to read the stand-up-statements to herself before her test to remind her to stay strong and stand up to OCD.

For You to Do

Jaden and her dad came up with some good stand-up-statements, but they could always use more.

If you were on Jaden's team, what stand-up-statement would you want Jaden to use? Write in the space provided:

_____

_____

_____

_____

_____

_____

_____

More for You to Do

Stand-up-statements can help you become stronger than OCD. What rule does OCD tell you to follow? Use this worksheet to write down what your OCD rule says, and then write down some stand-up-statements you can use to tell OCD that you are in charge. If you want to come up with even more stand-up-statements, you can download another copy at http://www.newharbinger.com/39782.

Stand-Up Statements Brainstorming Worksheet

My OCD rule says:

_____

_____

These statements can help me stand up to OCD:

_____

_____

_____

_____

_____

Stand-up statements will help you fight back against OCD. So don't forget to look back at your stand-up statements brainstorming worksheet.

Just Notice and Be Present

For You to Know

You learned earlier that trying to stop thinking about a sticky thought usually just makes it stick around more! Trying to distract yourself from your sticky thoughts often does not work either. Have you ever tried just noticing your sticky thoughts and letting them be? Sticky thoughts can be scary or annoying, but it's important to remember that they are *just thoughts*. Just because you have a sticky thought about something bad happening does not mean the bad thing will happen! Here are two strategies that work really well to deal with sticky thoughts that keep popping into your head:

1. Just notice.

2. Be present.

In the first step, when you *just notice*, you remind yourself that your sticky thought is just a thought, and you allow it be there. Many kids notice that just letting a sticky thought hang around makes that sticky thought go away or annoy them less. It's just like when a baseball player goes up to bat and hears members from the other team trash talking. They may tell the batter that he is no good and that he will strike out. The batter can get upset and try to get the other players to stop, but that probably won't work and will only distract the batter. The batter's best choice is to just notice the trash talk and keep playing. If you act like the batter, you will be less upset and annoyed by your sticky thoughts!

After you notice that your sticky thought is there, the next step is to *be present*. In this step, you try to bring your attention back to whatever you are doing, even when your sticky thought is bothering you. That is what the batter did when the other team was trash talking. He just kept playing! To help you be present, you can describe what you are doing. You might say to yourself, *My sticky thoughts are bugging me, but I will focus on what I am doing right now. Oh yeah…I am drawing a cover for my book report. I am going to focus on the different colors. I am now shading in the letters.* Being present can be hard at first, but like most things, it gets easier with practice!

Let us introduce Emma, who had some scary sticky thoughts but, with some help from her teacher, was able to handle them.

It was Monday morning and Emma was in her classroom learning about multiplication when she started having sticky images. Two days earlier, Emma had played a video game in which a scary image of a skeleton kept popping up. This skeleton image kept coming into her head as she tried to focus on math. Emma tried to shake the image out of her head, because it scared her so much, but the image kept coming back. She then tried to think about doing gymnastics, which was one of her favorite activities. Distracting herself helped a little, but Emma realized that she had missed the whole multiplication lesson. Emma felt very frustrated that her sticky images of the skeleton had prevented her from paying attention in class.

For You to Do

Emma's teacher, who was on her OCD team, taught her to just notice and be present when Emma had sticky thoughts or images in class. The statements below helped Emma just notice her sticky images:

Hi Sticky Image! I guess you came to say hello!

There is my sticky image of a skeleton trying to make me scared again!

My OCD is trying to make me think I have to distract myself. I can just notice my sticky image and allow it to be there.

If you have a sticky thought or image that bothers you, what can you say to help you just notice it? Put your thoughts in these thought bubbles:

More for You to Do

Emma was ready to practice being present in the classroom. Emma practiced describing what was actually happening in the room at the time instead of what her OCD was telling her to focus on. Over time, she found that her sticky thoughts of the skeleton bothered her less.

Here are some thoughts that helped Emma practice the strategy of being present:

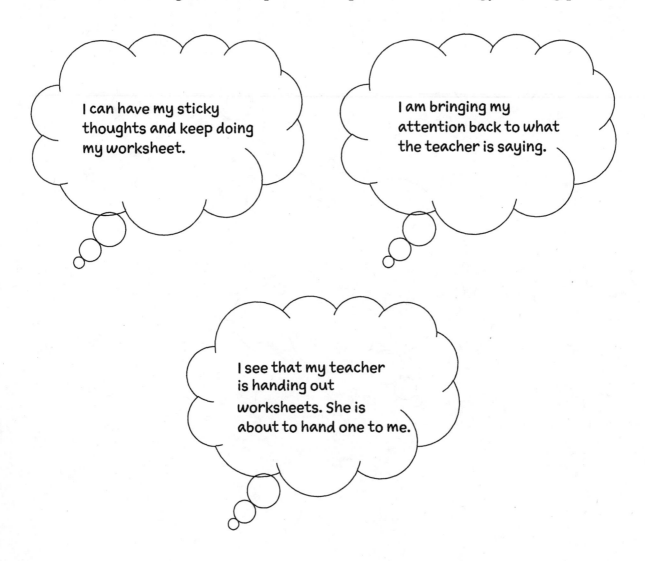

I can have my sticky thoughts and keep doing my worksheet.

I am bringing my attention back to what the teacher is saying.

I see that my teacher is handing out worksheets. She is about to hand one to me.

OCD Workbook for Kids

What thoughts can you say to yourself to practice this strategy of being present? Put your ideas into the thought bubbles below.

You did a great job learning how to just notice and be present. Keep practicing these skills whenever you notice your sticky thoughts or images.

Brave Challenges and Why We Do Them

For You to Know

By now, you already know a lot about OCD and how to start getting stronger than OCD. We think you're ready to learn two big skills that help lots of kids get stronger than OCD.

The fancy words for these skills are *exposure* and *ritual prevention*. But we call them *doing brave challenges* and *saying no to compulsions*. In this activity, we'll talk about doing brave challenges.

Doing a brave challenge is pretty simple. It involves doing something that makes you feel scared, worried, or "not right." You might be thinking, *Hold on! That sounds really hard!* Lots of kids feel that way. If brave challenges were easy, you would be doing them already! But we also know that when you do something scary or uncomfortable over and over again, it becomes less scary and uncomfortable (Jones 1924).

Here is an example: think of a TV show or movie that was a little scary for you. How did you feel after watching it? Now imagine watching that show or movie every day for a hundred days in a row. Would you still be as scared as you were the first time you saw it? Probably not. You might actually get a little bored of that show or movie, even if it was super scary at first!

Here is a story about a girl named Stella doing her first brave challenge:

Stella was really getting sick of living with OCD. The sticky thought that bothered her most was *What if I steal something when I am in a store?* Stella did not want to steal anything, but her sticky thoughts tried to convince her that she might steal something without knowing it. Her sticky thoughts bothered her so much that she tried to avoid going into stores whenever she could! When Stella had to go to the store with her mom, she forced herself to keep her hands in her pockets and made her mom tell her every few minutes that she had not stolen anything.

Stella learned that doing brave challenges could help her become stronger than her OCD. With her parents' help, Stella decided to do her first brave challenge. She went to the store with her mom and walked down one aisle by herself. The first time Stella tried this brave challenge, she felt really scared. It helped Stella to use a stand-up statement: "I don't need to follow OCD's rules anymore. Just because I have a sticky thought about stealing doesn't mean I will." After practicing several times, Stella was able to walk down a store aisle without feeling very scared at all.

We believe that you can do brave challenges too and that your brave challenges will get easier the more you do them!

For You to Do

Doing something scary or uncomfortable over and over again will make you feel less scared and uncomfortable about doing that thing. Here is a comic strip showing Stella facing her fear:

Think about something that was scary for you at first but became less scary for you the more often you did it. Here are some examples from other kids:

- Riding a bicycle

- Sleeping in the dark

- Eating a new food

Draw a picture of yourself the first time you did something scary and a second picture of yourself the 100th time you did the same thing. Write your thoughts for each picture in a thought bubble:

First Time You Did the Scary Thing	*100th Time You Did the Scary Thing*

More for You to Do

Imagine yourself doing something that OCD says is scary. This would be a brave challenge for you! If you have trouble coming up with a brave challenge, you can ask one of your team members for help. Draw a picture of yourself trying this brave challenge for the first time. Write in a thought bubble what you might be thinking. Then draw a picture of you trying that same brave challenge for the 100th time. Again, write in a thought bubble what you might be thinking when you try a brave challenge for the 100th time.

First Time You Try a Brave Challenge	*100th Time You Try the Brave Challenge*

Now that you have learned about brave challenges, you can move on to the next activity and start figuring out what brave challenges will help you!

Saying No to Compulsions

For You to Know

Along with completing brave challenges, saying no to compulsions will help you become stronger than OCD. Doing brave challenges and saying no to compulsions are two skills that work together to help you deal with OCD more easily. Here is an example of how it works.

Tara had sticky thoughts that wearing the color red would lead to someone in her family getting hurt. As a brave challenge, she wore a red skirt to school. She also said no to compulsions like calling her parents to make sure they were okay and covering her skirt with her jacket.

As you know, when you follow OCD's rules and do compulsions, it may help you feel a little better, but it also makes OCD stronger. Saying no to compulsions may feel really hard at first, but it will get easier the more you do it. And after a while, you will notice that you don't have the urge to follow OCD's rules nearly as much anymore.

Now that you have been tracking your compulsions for a little while, you are probably learning more about when, where, and how often you do them. It is time to put all of your good tracking work to use. It is time to start saying no to compulsions!

For You to Do

OCD may tell you that bad things are more likely to happen if you stop doing your compulsions. But remember, that's an OCD trap!

Think about a compulsion you do to make sure nothing bad will happen to you. Now write down the answers to these questions:

Do your family members do that compulsion? _____

Do your friends do that compulsion? _____

Do bad things happen to your friends and family more often than they happen to you?

_____

Probably not! That's because compulsions don't really protect you from bad things happening. They just make you feel a bit safer for a little while. But once you stop feeling safe, you need to do compulsions again, and again and again!

If your compulsions don't really work, why keep doing them? You can start saying no to your compulsions.

More for You to Do

We are going to walk you through the first steps of saying no to compulsions. We recommend you work with a parent or other team member to help you make a plan to start saying no.

Step 1: Ask yourself which compulsion you will say no to first. We usually suggest that kids pick one compulsion to start saying no to right away. Then, as you get the hang of it, you can start saying no to the rest of your compulsions. Tara chose "calling my mom to make sure she is okay" as the compulsion to practice saying no to first. You can look back to your compulsion checklist in activity 4 to decide which compulsion you want to say no to first. Remember, your job will be to try to not do this compulsion when OCD tells you to do it.

Step 2: Keep track of your progress. Keeping track will help remind you to practice saying no throughout the day. Plus, it will feel good to see your improvement from day to day! One way to keep track of your progress is to use a scorecard. Every time you say no to your compulsion, you place a tally mark next to "said no" on the scorecard. Every time you give in to OCD's rules, you place a tally mark next to "gave in."

Step 3: Tell your team about your saying-no-to-compulsions plan. We said it before and we'll say it again: saying no to compulsions is hard work! It can be very helpful to have people you trust to talk to when saying no feels super hard.

Tara kept track of her progress of saying no to her compulsion, using this scorecard.

Tara's Saying-No-to-Compulsions Scorecard

This week, I will practice saying no to this compulsion: **calling Mom to make sure she is okay.**

	SUNDAY	MONDAY	TUESDAY	WEDNESDAY	THURSDAY	FRIDAY	SATURDAY
Said no	II	III	III	IIIIIII	IIIII	IIIII	IIIIIIII
Gave in	IIIII	IIIII	IIIII	III	II	IIII	I

Now use this blank scorecard on the following page as a way to keep track of saying no to your compulsions.

Saying-No-to-Compulsions Scorecard

Write down a compulsion that you will practice saying no to.

This week, I will practice saying no to this compulsion: _____

	SUNDAY	MONDAY	TUESDAY	WEDNESDAY	THURSDAY	FRIDAY	SATURDAY
Said no							
Gave in							

Now every day for the next week, place a tally mark on the scorecard every time you said no to the compulsion and a tally mark every time you gave in by following the OCD rule.

If you want to use this saying-no-to-compulsions scorecard again, you can download another copy at http://www.newharbinger.com/39782.

Congratulations on starting to say no to your compulsions! We promise it will become easier over time, especially if you keep practicing!

Building Your
Brave-Challenge Tower

For You to Know

It's helpful to start doing brave challenges by practicing easier ones first rather than starting with the biggest challenge. Once you feel more comfortable doing easy brave challenges, you can start doing ones that feel a little harder and then continue to practice, doing more and more, until you meet your goal.

Easier brave challenges are ones that you feel pretty confident about doing even if they still feel a little scary. But how do you know which challenges will be easier to do than others? You can figure this out by building what we call a *brave-challenge tower*. Here's how Malcolm built his brave-challenge tower.

> Malcolm has sticky thoughts about needing to tap things four times. His OCD tells him that something bad might happen if he touches something without tapping it four times. Malcolm is most concerned about something bad happening to his parents, and so his OCD tells him to be sure to tap things belonging to his parents four times when he sees them. Malcolm worked with his mom to figure out brave challenges that would help him become stronger than OCD. Then they rated each brave challenge using a 1 to 10 scale, in which 1 was the easiest and 10 was the hardest challenge. After Malcolm rated his brave challenges, he wrote them on his brave-challenge tower.

This is what Malcolm's brave-challenge tower looked like:

Malcolm's Brave-Challenge Tower

Brave Challenge	Rating
Touch Dad's cellphone once and say "I hope this brings bad luck."	10
Touch Mom's purse just once and say "This might bring bad luck."	9
Touch the toothbrushes of every family member just once.	8
Touch all the forks and knives in the kitchen— no tapping at all!	7
Touch the doorknobs all around my house—no tapping at all!	5
Tap my schoolbooks and pencils twice.	3
Tap an apple in the supermarket three times and then buy it and eat it.	3
Tap an apple in the supermarket three times and leave it there.	2

As he was building his brave-challenge tower, Malcolm realized that touching things without tapping at all would be scarier than tapping something only three times. He also realized that saying things like "This will bring bad luck" when doing a brave challenge made it even scarier.

As you build your brave-challenge tower, you may feel like every brave challenge you think of will be *very* hard to do. A lot of kids feel this way. If your brave challenges feel too hard, it's important to break them down into easier challenges. Building your brave-challenge tower is a great activity to work on with members of your team—they can help you figure out some good brave challenges and help you rate them.

Once you've built your brave-challenge tower, you'll have a plan for taking on brave challenges. You'll just start at the bottom and work your way to the top of the tower.

For You to Do

Now it's time for you to make your brave-challenge tower. The first step is to work with your team to identify ten brave challenges. Don't worry about listing brave challenges for all the ways OCD bothers you. Many kids find it helpful to start listing things they wish they could do but their sticky thoughts say it's too scary or too hard. Those make great brave challenges! You can use Malcolm's brave-challenge tower as an example.

Your Brave Challenges

List your brave challenges here:

1. _____

2. _____

3. _____

4. _____

5. _____

6. _____

7. _____

8. _____

Now it's time to rate your brave challenges. Using a rating scale of 1 to 10, in which 1 is the easiest and 10 is the hardest, rate each of the brave challenges you just listed. You can look back at activity 9 if you need help on using a rating scale.

More for You to Do

Once you rate your challenges, you can build your brave-challenge tower! Start on the bottom line, writing down the brave challenge that you rated as easiest, and in the right-hand column, write down the rating that you gave it. Then add the next easiest brave challenge with its rating on the next line up and then the next easiest and so on. Keep doing this until you have all of your brave challenges on the brave-challenge tower with the hardest challenge of all at the top.

Once you've completed your tower, pat yourself on the back. That was a strong effort, and you have a great plan to keep getting stronger than OCD! If you want to build another brave-challenge tower again, you can download a copy at http://www.newharbinger.com/39782.

My Brave-Challenge Tower

Brave Challenge	Rating

Part 4

Brave Challenges

Getting Started with Brave Challenges

For You to Know

You have already learned a lot about OCD! You know about sticky thoughts and compulsions. You know that OCD's rules don't work. And you have some different tools to help you become stronger than OCD. So now it's time to practice, practice, practice!

To help you prepare for your first brave challenge, here is a story about Curtis's first (leadoff) brave challenge:

> After learning about how to stand up to OCD, Curtis decided he was ready to try his leadoff brave challenge. Curtis's OCD made him think that he might accidentally poison his family's food without knowing it. Because of these sticky thoughts, Curtis did not touch any food that his family might eat, and he often ate in a different room from his family. He also checked with his parents after they ate to make sure they were not poisoned.
>
> Curtis understood that his first brave challenge was supposed to feel hard enough to bother his OCD but not so hard that he would be unable to do it. With his parents' help, he decided his first brave challenge would be to touch sandwiches that his family members planned to eat for lunch. Curtis had rated this brave challenge as a 4 on his brave-challenge tower, which told him that this brave challenge would be scary but not too scary.

Here's what you need to know to prepare for your own leadoff brave challenge.

Your Goal

It's important to set a goal. Here are some guidelines for brave-challenge goals:

Brave-challenge goals should be in your control. You can control whether you touch a doorknob that you think is germy. So "I will touch a doorknob even if I think it's germy" is a good goal! You cannot control if you get sick the day after you touch that doorknob. So "I will touch a doorknob without getting sick tomorrow" is not a good goal.

Brave-challenge goals should be about *doing*, **not** *feeling*. If you have sticky thoughts about needing to understand everything you read, skipping a page of your school reading is a good goal! But trying to feel just fine about it when you skip that reading is not a good goal.

What You Will Need with You

Just like a softball player needs a mitt and an artist needs a paintbrush, you may need certain materials to complete your brave challenge. Curtis needed to have his family around, and he needed some sandwiches for them to eat. If you don't have everything you need, ask a parent or other team member to help you.

Your Stand-Up Statements

Stand-up statements can help you stay strong when completing your brave challenge. We recommend coming up with one or two stand-up statements that you think will help before taking on a brave challenges. You can always look back to activity 11 for examples.

Your Brave-Challenge Schedule

Finally, you need to decide how many times you will practice your leadoff brave challenge this week. The more you practice, the stronger you will get! We encourage kids to practice each brave challenge three or four times a week. But if you can practice every day, that's even better!

Keep Saying No to Compulsions

Brave challenges are most helpful when you can say no to compulsions during the challenge. When you prepare for a brave challenge, think about which compulsions OCD will tell you to do, so you will be prepared to say no!

For You to Do

Are you ready? No one ever feels 100 percent ready to try something new. If you are feeling scared and not sure if you want to try your brave challenge, take some time to review your reasons for getting stronger than OCD, which you wrote down in activity 1. Then plan for your first brave challenge. If you think you are ready, you can plan for your brave challenge by filling out this worksheet.

Planning Your Brave Challenge

For your leadoff brave challenge, first choose a brave challenge that is toward the bottom of your brave-challenge tower (see activity 15). Write your leadoff brave challenge here:

_____

Think of what you will need to have with you. Which people or what things do you need to complete your brave challenge?

_____

_____

Think of some stand-up statements for your first brave challenge. Write them down.

_____

_____

Schedule your brave challenge. How many times will you practice your brave challenge this week?

1   2   3   4   5   6   7

More for You to Do

Now it's time to practice! You can use a brave-challenge scorecard to keep track of your leadoff brave challenge. Here is Curtis's scorecard.

Curtis's Brave-Challenge Scorecard

Brave challenge: **Touch each sandwich with my fingers**

Goal for this brave challenge: **Allow my family members to eat their sandwiches after I touch them**

Stand-up statements: **OCD doesn't tell me what to do! I want to eat with my family, not with OCD!**

Draw a star under each day that you practice your brave challenge!

SUNDAY	MONDAY	TUESDAY	WEDNESDAY	THURSDAY	FRIDAY	SATURDAY
★	★		★		★	★

Now it's your turn. Use the scorecard on the next page to keep track of your leadoff brave challenge!

Getting Started with Brave Challenges

Brave-Challenge Scorecard

Fill in the blanks.

Your brave challenge: _____

Your goal for this brave challenge: _____

_____

Your stand-up statements: _____

_____

Draw a star under each day that you practice your brave challenge!

SUNDAY	MONDAY	TUESDAY	WEDNESDAY	THURSDAY	FRIDAY	SATURDAY

To use this brave-challenge scorecard again, you can download another copy at http://www.newharbinger.com/39782.

Excellent job getting started with brave challenges! The next five activities will guide you in doing brave challenges for specific types of sticky thoughts. Not every activity may focus on *your* type of sticky thoughts, but we recommend you read each activity to learn about all the ways you can get stronger than OCD!

Get Dirty! Exposure Ideas for Contamination Sticky Thoughts

Activity 17

For You to Know

It is very common for kids to have sticky thoughts that they might get germs on them. Other kids may worry about dirt, blood, poison, urine, poop, or other yucky things. We call these *contamination sticky thoughts* because OCD's rules focus on not getting contaminated by something or some substance.

> Dante noticed that he was having a lot of sticky thoughts about germs being on his books, pencils, and lunch box. Dante was afraid he would get sick and possibly get a stomach bug if he touched something with other kids' germs on it. Dante started using hand sanitizer over and over again while at school and avoided eating lunch at school. When he got home every day, he washed his hands a lot until he felt like the germs were off. Dante's hands became red and chapped from all the washing. Dante also avoided opening his notebooks and textbooks, because they might have germs on them, which made it very hard for him to complete his homework. He knew his OCD was starting to really interfere with his life.

Do you ever have sticky thoughts like Dante's? If so, here are some things you should know about contamination sticky thoughts.

Contamination sticky thoughts are not all the same. Some kids have sticky thoughts about getting sick if they touch yucky things, and other kids have sticky thoughts about getting other people sick. Other kids have sticky thoughts that they will just feel really gross if they touch certain things. You may have one type of contamination sticky thought, or you may have more than one type.

Contamination sticky thoughts usually lead to washing compulsions. When kids have sticky thoughts about having germs or dirt on them, they usually do compulsions in which they keep washing their hands a certain number of times or for a certain amount of time or until it feels "just right." They may have to wipe a lot after using the bathroom, because they are afraid of having urine or poop on them.

Contamination sticky thoughts might lead to confessing or reassurance compulsions. Kids with contamination sticky thoughts might ask their parents questions over and over about whether certain people or things are clean or dirty. They might even confess that they touched something, and look to see their parents' reactions.

Remember, the best way to get stronger than OCD is with brave challenges! Here is a list of some common contamination sticky thoughts and what we call *get-dirty brave challenges* that kids often do to get stronger than these sticky thoughts:

If you have sticky thoughts about...	Then these brave challenges may help...
Having germs on you	• Touch something sticky like honey or glue and set a timer on for a certain amount of time that you agree to not wash your hands. • Go around your house touching "dirty" or "germy" things without washing your hands. • Rinse your hands with water only and do not use soap. • Eat a piece of candy that touched something "germy."
Feeling "dirty"	• Sit in a "dirty" place and play a game. • Walk barefoot in "dirty" places. • Play on a playground that has "dirty" stuff near it, and then have a snack.
Not wiping enough to get the urine or poop off of you	• Wipe with the wrong hand (if you are a righty, wipe with your left hand). • Put a drop of water in your underwear and wear them.
A friend or family member being sick or "dirty"	• Have this person make you a snack. • Give this person a hug or shake hands with this person. • Touch this person's clothing. • Have lunch with this person. • Watch TV while sitting next to this person.

Remember, you will need to practice these brave challenges over and over to get used to them. The more you practice, the easier it will get!

For You to Do

If you have contamination sticky thoughts, try a get-dirty brave challenge! You can use the list on the previous page to help you come up with ideas. Don't forget to ask a parent or another trusted adult to help you! Use a brave-challenge scorecard to keep track of your challenge.

Get-Dirty Brave-Challenge Scorecard

Fill in the blanks.

Your brave challenge: _____

Your goal for this brave challenge: _____

_____

Use one or more of these stand-up statements, or come up with your own:

OCD's rules do not keep me clean—they just waste my time.

Feeling dirty isn't the same as being dirty.

I would rather deal with germs than live with OCD.

Draw a star under each day that you practice your brave challenge!

SUNDAY	MONDAY	TUESDAY	WEDNESDAY	THURSDAY	FRIDAY	SATURDAY

To use this brave-challenge scorecard again, you can download another copy at http://www.newharbinger.com/39782.

More for You to Do

Your other job this week is to continue to say no to compulsions. Here are some compulsions that kids do when contamination sticky thoughts bother them:

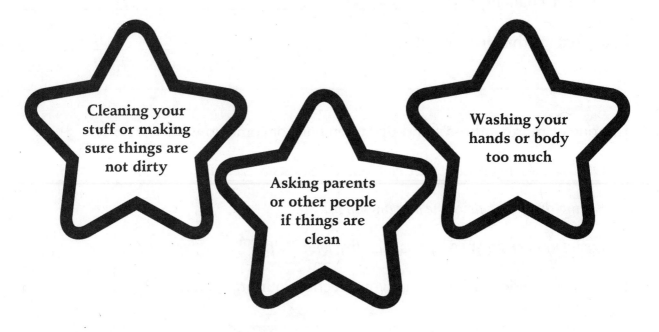

Do you do any compulsions like these? If so, write them down here, and try to resist them as much as possible from now on.

I will say no to these compulsions from now on:

_____

_____

_____

Keep up the great work—you are getting stronger than OCD every day!

For You to Know

Many kids have sticky thoughts that they will be responsible for something bad happening to them or someone else. We call these *safety sticky thoughts* because OCD's rules focus on keeping everyone safe. Here's an example.

> Amelia's most upsetting sticky thought was that she might be responsible for a fire burning down her house. She worried that if she left a light bulb on for too long, it would explode and cause a fire. Amelia went around her house a lot to make sure that lights were off in empty rooms. She sometimes turned off lights when her family was in a room. Amelia's brother started calling her "the light police," which really bothered her. Sticky thoughts also upset Amelia at night, and she usually got out of bed three or four times each night to make sure the lights in her house were off.

Do you ever have any safety sticky thoughts? If so, here are some things you should know about them:

Safety sticky thoughts can make you worry about stuff that is not your responsibility. Sticky thoughts usually make you think you're responsible for things that you don't really need to worry about! Most kids are not in charge of making sure their house is safe. That job is for moms and dads and other adults!

Safety sticky thoughts usually lead to checking compulsions. When you have safety sticky thoughts, you may check that doors in your house are locked, that the oven is turned off, or that home computers are turned off. You may ask your parents or other adults if everything is okay.

Here is a list of some common safety sticky thoughts and what we call *live-with-risk brave challenges* that kids often do to get stronger than these sticky thoughts:

If you have sticky thoughts about...	Then these brave challenges may help...
Your house door being unlocked	• Spend some time in your home with the door unlocked (if an adult is home and agrees to this plan). • Have an adult quickly lock the front door without the adult looking before leaving the house. • Read stories or watch movies about burglars robbing homes. Have your parents help you choose one.
Your oven being left on	• Cook or bake with an adult and have the adult be in charge of turning off the oven. • Have an adult quickly turn the stove or oven on and off before leaving the house.
Starting a fire in your house	• Have an adult light some candles in the house; have the adult be in charge of blowing the candles out. • Leave lights on in all of the rooms of your house.
Accidentally poisoning someone	• Make food for your family once a day for a week. • Prepare food for someone and have a spray cleaner nearby on the counter. • Serve food that is expired by one or two days to an adult.

If you think any of these brave challenges can help you get stronger than OCD, add them to your brave-challenge tower!

For You to Do

If you have safety sticky thoughts, try a live-with-risk brave challenge! You can use the list on the previous page to help you come up with ideas for your brave challenge. Don't forget to ask a parent or another trusted adult to help you! Use a brave-challenge scorecard to keep track of your challenge:

Live-with-Risk Brave-Challenge Scorecard

Fill in the blanks.

Your brave challenge: _____

Your goal for this brave challenge: _____

_____

Use one or more of these stand-up-statements, or come up with your own:

OCD's rules do not keep me safe—they just waste my time.

Thinking about something bad happening doesn't mean it will happen.

I would rather live with a little risk than live with OCD.

OCD is just trying to make me upset, but I won't let it.

Draw a star under each day that you practice your brave challenge!

SUNDAY	MONDAY	TUESDAY	WEDNESDAY	THURSDAY	FRIDAY	SATURDAY

To use this brave-challenge scorecard again, you can download another copy at http://www.newharbinger.com/39782.

More for You to Do

Your other job this week is to continue to say no to compulsions. Here are some compulsions that kids do when safety sticky thoughts bother them:

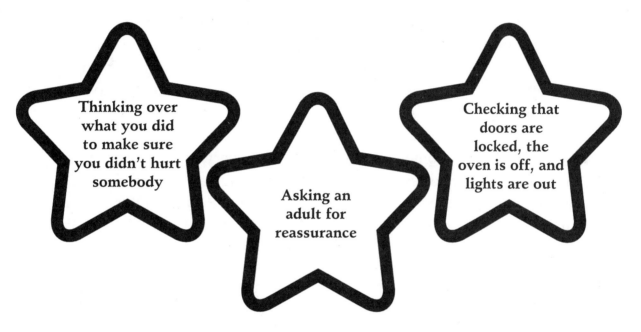

Thinking over what you did to make sure you didn't hurt somebody

Asking an adult for reassurance

Checking that doors are locked, the oven is off, and lights are out

Do you do any compulsions like these? If so, write them down here, and try to resist them as much as possible from now on.

I will say no to these compulsions from now on:

_____

_____

_____

Keep up the great work—you are getting stronger than OCD every day!

Make Mistakes! Exposure
Ideas for Being-Perfect Sticky Thoughts

For You to Know

Many kids with OCD have sticky thoughts about doing things perfectly or making mistakes. We call these *being-perfect sticky thoughts*. Here is an example:

When doing his homework, TJ has sticky thoughts that the letters he wrote needed to look perfect so that his teacher could understand his writing. He was afraid that he would lose points on his homework if his writing was not perfect. TJ often rewrote letters five or six times until they looked perfect! TJ also had sticky thoughts that he made mistakes on his work, and he reviewed his math homework over and over to make sure he did not make a mistake. TJ's homework took him hours every night. Even worse, rewriting his work and reviewing his answers over and over made him very angry, and he often yelled at his parents when they tried to help him. On many nights, TJ went to bed without finishing his homework, because it took too long.

Do you have thoughts like TJ's? If so, here are some things you should know about being-perfect sticky thoughts:

Being-perfect sticky thoughts make you think that you need to be perfect all the time. But nobody's perfect! We all make mistakes. Even the best baseball players get outs more than they get hits. Being-perfect sticky thoughts may try to convince you that you can be perfect, but that's impossible.

Being-perfect sticky thoughts and redoing compulsions do not lead to perfect results! Most kids with being-perfect sticky thoughts give up before doing something perfectly, because doing the same thing over and over is *so* frustrating. Just another example of OCD's rules not working!

Here is a list of some common being-perfect sticky thoughts and what we call *make-mistakes brave challenges* that kids often do to get stronger than these sticky thoughts:

If you have sticky thoughts about...	Then these brave challenges may help...
Doing your homework perfectly	• Make a mistake on a homework assignment on purpose. • Leave a homework question blank. • Give yourself a time limit to complete a homework assignment, and do not go over the time limit.
Writing letters perfectly	• Include a sentence full of messy letters on a homework assignment. • Display a sign with messy handwriting on your bedroom door, refrigerator, or school desk. • Write with the hand you normally do not use for writing.
Making sure you read something completely	• Practice reading each word in a book or website only once. Read out loud if it helps. • Speed-read through a favorite book or website. • Skip one sentence on every page or every paragraph.
Saying prayers perfectly	*Check with your parents, or a priest, rabbi, or imam, before doing these brave challenges, so they can help you fight OCD while also following the rules of your religion:* • Say each word of your prayer only once. • Skip one word in a prayer you say. • Practice saying your prayers quickly.

If you have sticky thoughts about...	Then these brave challenges may help...
Making sure your clothes and hair look perfect	• Wear your hair very messy or out of style. • Wear mismatching clothes. • Place a stain on your clothes and go out in public.
Making sure people understand you perfectly when you say something	• Speak quickly and do not repeat yourself. • Mumble your words on purpose. • Add a nonsense word to something you're saying, so it doesn't make 100 percent sense.

Remember, these brave challenges will feel hard at first, but the more you practice, the easier they will get!

For You to Do

If you have being-perfect sticky thoughts, try a make-mistakes brave challenge! You can use the list on the previous page to help you come up with ideas. Don't forget to ask a parent or another trusted adult to help you! Use a brave-challenge scorecard to keep track of your challenge.

Make-Mistakes Brave-Challenge Scorecard

Fill in the blanks.

Your brave challenge: _____

Your goal for this brave challenge: _____

_____

Use one or more of these stand-up-statements, or come up with your own:

My work does not need to be perfect to be good enough.

Nobody's perfect, so why even try?

Trying to be perfect just makes things worse!

Perfect is boring—I'm perfectly imperfect!

Draw a star under each day that you practice your brave challenge!

SUNDAY	MONDAY	TUESDAY	WEDNESDAY	THURSDAY	FRIDAY	SATURDAY

To use this brave-challenge scorecard again, you can download another copy at http://www.newharbinger.com/39782.

OCD Workbook for Kids

More for You to Do

Your other job this week is to continue to say no to compulsions. Here are some compulsions that kids do when being-perfect sticky thoughts bother them:

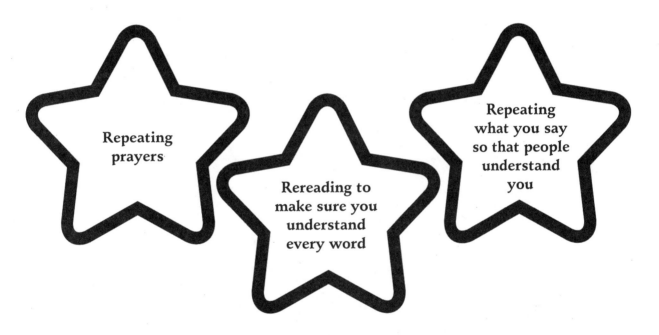

Repeating prayers

Rereading to make sure you understand every word

Repeating what you say so that people understand you

Do you do any compulsions like these? If so, write them down here, and try to resist them as much as possible from now on.

I will say no to these compulsions from now on:

_____

_____

_____

Keep up the great work—you are getting stronger than OCD every day!

It's Just a Thought!
Exposure Ideas for "Bad" Sticky Thoughts

> **Note for parents:** Some of the content in this activity focuses on topics that may not be suitable for your child. We include this content because many children do experience obsessions related to forbidden or taboo topics. Please preview this activity before your child reads it. If you decide the content is suitable for your child, we encourage you to review the activity with your child, so you can answer any questions and provide your family's perspective on the subject matter.

For You to Know

Some kids have sticky thoughts about things that just seem wrong or bad to think about. We call these *"bad" sticky thoughts*. These sticky thoughts are usually about hurting someone else on purpose, doing something sinful or that will upset God, or doing something sexual. Here's an example:

Whenever Veronica walked outside, she experienced a very upsetting sticky thought: that she would suddenly have the urge to trip people who walked past her. Veronica did not want to trip anyone, but her sticky thoughts would say, *How do you know for sure? Maybe you really do want to trip someone?* The thoughts bothered Veronica so much that she often avoided taking family walks and begged her parents to drive her to school, even though her school was only two blocks away.

Do you have sticky thoughts like Veronica's? If so, here are some things you should know about these thoughts:

Kids who have "bad" sticky thoughts do not want to do the things they think about. But they are afraid they might do them even though they don't want to. Some kids worry that thinking about a bad thing means they really want to do it. So they try to avoid having these thoughts altogether.

"Bad" sticky thoughts are really hard to discuss. Kids often feel embarrassed to share these sticky thoughts or are afraid that adults may be mad at them for thinking about bad things.

Everyone has bad thoughts sometimes. We all think about doing things that are forbidden, illegal, or just plain wrong. We cannot control the thoughts we have, which is why there is nothing wrong with having bad thoughts.

Here is a list of some common "bad" sticky thoughts and what we call *it's-just-a-thought brave challenges* that kids often do to get stronger than these sticky thoughts. Before trying these brave challenges, it's important to review them with an adult member of your team.

If you have sticky thoughts about...	*Then these brave challenges may help...*
Hurting a family member	• Sit or stand near that family member for fifteen minutes. • Gently place your hands on an adult and keep them there for a minute. • Write "I want to hurt my family" twenty times in a row.
Causing a horrible thing to happen, like someone dying, a fire, or an earthquake	• Wish over and over that the horrible thing happens (*I wish that my grandpa dies* or *I wish that there is a tornado in Oklahoma*). • Write "I hope that ____happens" twenty times in a row (filling in the blank).
Stealing something from a store	• Hold an item in your hand as you walk around the store.
Saying curse words out loud	• Whisper or silently say curse words in public. • Say curse words out loud at home with family members. • Play curse-word Hangman.
Acting sexually toward a family member	• Spend alone time with the family member. • Hug the family member once per day. • Sit next to the family member on the couch while watching a movie.
Going to hell	• Read Bible stories describing hell. • Complete a word search with words related to hell. • Say prayers incorrectly.

It can feel especially scary to try these brave challenges. Working with a team member can help make them easier!

For You to Do

If you have "bad" sticky thoughts, try an it's-just-a-thought brave challenge! You can use the list on the previous page to help you come up with ideas for your brave challenge. Don't forget to ask a parent or another trusted adult to help you! Use a brave-challenge scorecard to keep track of your challenge:

It's-Just-a-Thought Brave-Challenge Scorecard

Fill in the blanks.

Your brave challenge:_____

Your goal for this brave challenge: _____

_____

Use one or more of these stand-up-statements, or come up with your own:

A thought is just a thought—it doesn't mean anything about me!

I trust myself to act the right way, no matter what OCD says!

I won't let OCD tell me what to do.

Draw a star under each day that you practice your brave challenge!

SUNDAY	MONDAY	TUESDAY	WEDNESDAY	THURSDAY	FRIDAY	SATURDAY

To use this brave-challenge scorecard again, you can download another copy at http://www.newharbinger.com/39782.

More for You to Do

Your other job this week is to continue to say no to compulsions.

Here are some compulsions that kids do when "bad" sticky thoughts bother them:

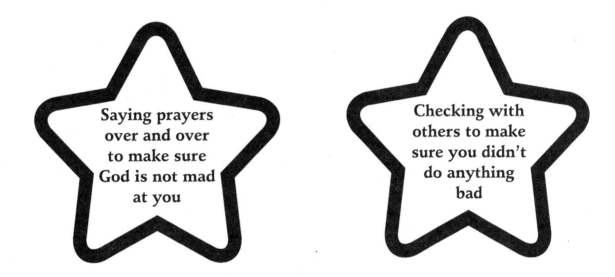

Saying prayers over and over to make sure God is not mad at you

Checking with others to make sure you didn't do anything bad

Do you do any compulsions like these? If so, write them down here, and try to resist them as much as possible from now on.

I will say no to these compulsions from now on:

_____

_____

_____

Keep up the great work—you are getting stronger than OCD every day!

Do It Wrong! Exposure
Ideas for Not-Right Sticky Thoughts

For You to Know

Some kids have sticky thoughts about things being "not right" or "off." Here's an example:

> Terrence felt uncomfortable unless his bedroom was arranged in a certain way. He needed to have his bed made perfectly and his pillows arranged in a very specific order before he would feel comfortable again. Terrence also needed to arrange his action figures from tallest to smallest, and his shoes needed to all face the same way on his bedroom floor, or else he would feel uncomfortable. Soon Terrence was spending an hour each night arranging things in his room to make sure he felt comfortable before going to bed!

Do you ever have sticky thoughts like these? We call these *not-right sticky thoughts*. If you have these sticky thoughts, here are some things you should know about them:

Your not-right sticky thought may be just an icky or uncomfortable feeling. It may not feel like a thought at all, but not-right sticky thoughts are just like other sticky thoughts in one important way—they try to trick you into thinking you need to do compulsions to be okay.

Not-right sticky thoughts usually lead to compulsions to make the feeling go away. Kids with not-right sticky thoughts may need to arrange their bedroom, toys, or book bag in a certain way. Or they may need to tap or touch something over and over or do something an odd or even number of times.

Remember that sticky thoughts go away on their own, even if you don't follow OCD's rules to do compulsions. The same goes for feeling not right—that feeling will go away with time, no matter what. So your job is to practice brave challenges that make you have not-right sticky thoughts, and to say no to compulsions.

Here is a list of some common not-right sticky thoughts and what we call *do-it-wrong brave challenges* that kids often do to get stronger than these sticky thoughts:

If you have sticky thoughts about...	*Then these brave challenges may help...*
Your clothes, toys, or other things being out of order	• Place your stuff in the wrong order when you go to school or before you leave the house. • Place one thing out of order and plan to keep it there for at least a week. • Ask a team member to move your stuff out of order without telling you. You are not allowed to rearrange things your team member messes up!
Needing to touch or tap something over and over until it feels "right"	• Pick a time each day when you practice touching something only once. Try to extend this time every few days! • Play a game in which a team member gives you a point for every time you touch objects the first time and resist retouching or tapping it. Ten points earns you a reward!
Needing to do something an even number of times	• Play the Odd Olympics! Create a series of tasks that you will practice doing an odd number of times. Take an odd number of bites of food, take an odd number of steps before stopping, or blink an odd number of times. (If your sticky thoughts tell you to do things an odd number of times, you can do these tasks an *even* amount of times.)

Remember, you will need to practice these brave challenges over and over to get used to them. It will feel hard at first, but the more you practice, the easier it will get!

For You to Do

If you have not-right sticky thoughts, try a do-it-wrong brave challenge! You can use the list on the previous page to help you come up with ideas for your brave challenge. Don't forget to ask a parent or another trusted adult to help you! Use a brave-challenge scorecard to keep track of your challenge.

Do-It-Wrong Brave-Challenge Scorecard

Fill in the blanks.

Your brave challenge: _____

Your goal for this brave challenge: _____

_____

Use one or more of these stand-up-statements, or come up with your own:

I can handle feeling not right for a little while.

I would rather feel a little uncomfortable than do everything OCD says!

I'm sick of listening to OCD—I'm the boss!

Draw a star under each day that you practice your brave challenge!

SUNDAY	MONDAY	TUESDAY	WEDNESDAY	THURSDAY	FRIDAY	SATURDAY

To use this brave-challenge scorecard again, you can download another copy at http://www.newharbinger.com/39782.

Skills to Help Children Manage Obsessive Thoughts and Compulsive Behaviors

More for You to Do

Your other goal this week is to say no to compulsions when your not-right sticky thoughts bother you. Here are some compulsions that other kids do when not-right sticky thoughts bother them:

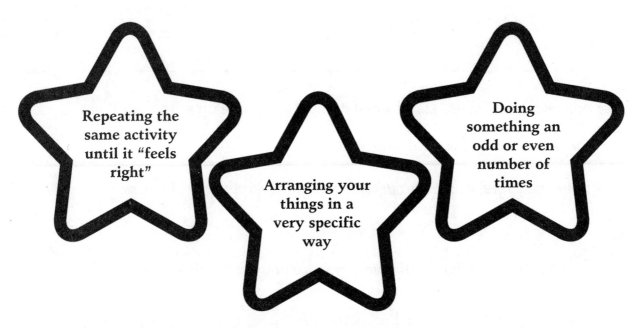

Repeating the same activity until it "feels right"

Arranging your things in a very specific way

Doing something an odd or even number of times

Do you do any compulsions like these? If so, write them down here, and try to resist them as much as possible from now on.

I will say no to these compulsions from now on:

_____

_____

_____

Keep up the great work—you are getting stronger than OCD every day!

Keep Climbing Your Brave-Challenge Tower

For You to Know

The purpose of this activity is to help you keep climbing your brave-challenge tower and facing those brave challenges that may have seemed *super scary* when you first started working on your OCD. If you're like many kids, you may notice that the brave challenges you rated as very hard may not feel so hard anymore!

Steve had sticky thoughts that he needed to walk through doorways over and over again until it felt "just right." He was afraid that he would feel uncomfortable all day if he did not follow OCD's rules. Before he started brave challenges, Steve spent more than an hour each day walking in and out of doorways. He would think, *What a waste of time!* With help from his team, Steve began walking just once through different doorways in his home. However, it was very hard for him to walk only once through the front door; he rated this brave challenge as a 9 ½ on his brave-challenge tower.

One afternoon, Steve's dad asked Steve if he was ready to be a brave-challenge super hero and try to walk through the front door just once without repeating. Steve immediately felt nervous but then realized that walking through other doorways was becoming much easier. Steve and his father reviewed his brave-challenge tower, and Steve realized that most of his brave challenges were not as scary as they used to be. This helped him feel more ready to take on his hardest brave challenge. When Steve first practiced walking through his front door only once, he felt super uncomfortable, and he became nervous that he would keep feeling uncomfortable all day long. The uncomfortable feeling lasted a while, but by dinnertime Steve realized he was not feeling so bad anymore.

Activity 22 Keep Climbing Your Brave-Challenge Tower

Completing brave challenges is just like learning any other skill. The more you practice, the easier it gets, and the more you feel ready to take on more challenging skills! For example, when kids start learning to play an instrument, just playing single notes can be very hard. But with practice, playing those notes becomes easier, and kids feel ready to start playing whole songs. Can you think of something that was hard to do at first but now seems easy?

For You to Do

After practicing brave challenges for a while, Steve and his dad gave new ratings to the brave challenges on his tower. Take a look at Steve's brave-challenge tower with his new ratings:

Steve's Brave-Challenge Tower

Brave Challenge	Rating	
Walk through house front door just once	~~9½~~	7
Walk through bedroom door just once	~~8~~	5
Walk through school entrance just once	~~7~~	5
Walk through bathroom doors just once	~~7~~	5
Walk through sister's bedroom door just once	~~4~~	1
Walk through store entrances just once	~~4~~	1
Walk through doorways in Grandpa's house just once	~~3~~	1
Step into car just once	~~3~~	0

Now go back to your brave-challenge tower in activity 15 and review the ratings that you gave your brave challenges. Would you give them the same ratings today? Which brave challenges are feeling easier now? Update the ratings for any brave challenges that feel easier now!

More for You to Do

Be a brave-challenge super hero like Steve! Choose one item from your brave-challenge tower that you never thought you would be able to face. Put a plan together with your team to face this challenge. You can use a brave-challenge scorecard to help you plan!

And keep on saying no to your compulsions!

Enlisting Your Team to Help with Brave Challenges

For You to Know

Completing brave challenges is an important part of becoming stronger than your OCD, but it can sometimes be difficult to do this work all by yourself. Your team members (parents, teachers, therapists, or other supportive adults) can help you work on your brave challenges. Here's a story about a girl named Layla who asked her mom to be part of her team.

Layla had sticky thoughts that if she heard or thought about a curse word, something bad would happen to her. When Layla had these sticky thoughts, she asked her mom if something bad would happen. If Layla's mom didn't reassure her with "Everything will be okay," then Layla would keep asking until her mom followed OCD's rules. When Layla's mom learned that doing compulsions makes OCD worse, she realized she needed to stop reassuring Layla.

Your team members can do certain things to help you with your brave challenges. For example, Layla and her mom decided that her mom could help by

1. Cheering Layla on when she does brave challenges

2. Refusing to play by OCD's rules (even when it is really hard)

3. Helping Layla plan brave challenges

Layla's first brave challenge was reading a curse word and saying it out loud in a room by herself. After she said the curse word, she was not supposed to ask her mom if everything would be okay. Layla really wanted the first brave challenge to be successful and wasn't sure she could do it. Layla's mom cheered her on and encouraged her to first whisper the curse word and then try it in a loud voice. This helped Layla feel more confident, and she succeeded with her first brave challenge.

For You to Do

Think of some things that your team members can do to help you with your brave challenges. For example, hearing her mom cheer her on made Layla feel stronger. Layla's mom cheered her on with these supportive statements:

I know you can be stronger than your OCD.

The nervous feeling will go away on its own!

Doing compulsions only makes OCD Stronger!

You can do this! Tell OCD that you aren't going to listen to its rules.

What are some things that you want one or more of your team members to say to you? In the speech bubbles below write what you want your team members to say to cheer you on.

More for You to Do

Review your brave-challenge tower with a team member, so you can see which brave challenges will be easier with your team's support. Place a star next to any challenges that you might need some support or help with. For parents and other caregivers, A Caregiver's Guide to Brave Challenges appears at the end of this book.

Now that you have spoken with members of your team about ways they can help you become stronger than OCD, try out some brave challenges with one of your team members. The more you practice standing up to OCD, the stronger you will feel!

Part 5

Staying Strong

Activity 24 Refueling Your Mind and Body (Sleep, Eating, Exercise)

For You to Know

This activity discusses the importance of taking care of your body, so you can have enough energy to become stronger than OCD. People need fuel to make their bodies run, just like cars need gasoline to fuel their engines. Instead of gasoline, we need to get enough sleep, eat healthy food, and exercise. Doing these things helps us have enough energy to stay stronger than OCD!

Getting the right amount of sleep gives you energy to complete difficult brave challenges. Not getting enough sleep can make kids more irritable and less ready to take on OCD. Another way you can fuel your body is to eat healthy foods throughout the day. Finally, scientists have found that exercising can help reduce anxiety (de Bruin, van der Zwan, and Bögels 2016). Whether it is running, swimming, or basketball, any form of physical exercise can help reduce stress and may lower anxiety too!

Here is a story about how a twelve-year-old named Mark who was having difficulty coping with OCD.

> Mark's OCD made him believe that all his letters and numbers had to look a certain way on the page. If he saw a letter or a number that didn't look quite right, OCD told him he needed to redo it. Sometimes OCD made him redo his writing assignments three or four times. To relieve his stress, Mark stayed up late at night playing video games. He found that playing video games calmed him down, but he was not getting enough sleep. When it was time to work on brave challenges, Mark told his mom that he was too tired to do them and he just wanted to get his homework done so that he

could get back to his video games. Instead of eating dinner with the family, Mark ate a granola bar while he did his homework. He felt really hungry while doing homework, which made it difficult to say no to his rewriting compulsions. Mark's mom grew concerned that Mark was not getting any exercise, because he spent most of his free time either doing homework or playing video games. Mark was following OCD's rules, because he did not have the energy to complete brave challenges and say no to compulsions.

What changes could Mark make to give him the energy to stand up to OCD?

For You to Do

Look again at Mark's story. Are there changes in his sleeping, eating, and exercise habits that he could make to be healthier and give him more energy? Can you list some here?

1. _____

2. _____

3. _____

Eating healthier, getting more sleep, and exercising will help Mark feel stronger when OCD bothers him!

More for You to Do

Just like with Mark, there may be ways for you to fuel your mind and body better!

Are there any changes you can make to your life to give you enough fuel to stand up to OCD? List them here:

I can improve my sleep by _____

I can eat healthy by _____

I can stay active by _____

By making changes that fuel your mind and body better, you will have more energy to stand up to OCD. It can sometimes be difficult to stick to these changes, but the more you keep it up, the easier it will get!

Activity 25 What to Do When OCD Follows You to School

For You to Know

Many kids notice that OCD follows them to school! When this happens, it can be difficult to pay attention, stay in your seat, or complete work on time. Sometimes it can be helpful to talk to your teacher or school counselor about OCD, but *the decision to talk to school staff about OCD should be made with your parents or caregivers.* If you do decide to speak with your teacher or counselor, that person can help you plan and complete brave challenges, say no to compulsions, and reward you for standing up to OCD.

Here is a story about how Courtney, her parents, and her teacher worked as a team when OCD bothered Courtney at school.

> OCD would often make Courtney doubt herself when she was in class. She kept asking her teacher, Mrs. Reed, if the answers on her math worksheets were correct. Courtney's questions distracted the other kids in the classroom. OCD also told Courtney that she needed to know the answers to any questions that popped into her head. For example, when she saw a cloud in the sky, she needed to ask whether her class would have outdoor recess if it started to rain. Mrs. Reed was very confused about why Courtney kept asking questions, and sent a note home to her parents. So Courtney and her parents had a family meeting to discuss how to talk to Mrs. Reed about Courtney's OCD and ask if she would be willing to be part of Courtney's team. This is what Courtney and her parents wanted Mrs. Reed to know:

Hi Mrs. Reed,

I have OCD. OCD stands for obsessive-compulsive disorder. This means that a part of my brain tells me to follow rules so that I won't feel nervous. Sometimes OCD tells me that I need to know the answers to my questions or I will feel really nervous. I have a hard time with this nervous feeling, so I try to avoid it by getting answers to my questions (this is my compulsion). This only makes OCD worse! I noticed that I am asking about ten questions a day in class. I want to ask fewer questions in class. My parents and I were wondering if we could start a system that if I ask only five questions a day, you put a star on a chart that goes home each day. My parents will then reward me at home with screen time.

Thanks for your help!

Courtney

Courtney, her parents, and Mrs. Reed had a private meeting at school to discuss Courtney's OCD. Mrs. Reed agreed to use the system of keeping a chart with stars to help Courtney stand up to OCD and to send the chart home with Courtney every day. She also agreed to keep Courtney's OCD private and agreed that the other students did not have to know about the chart. Mrs. Reed and Courtney's parents were very proud of Courtney for working with her team to become stronger than OCD.

For You to Do

Is OCD following you to school too? If so, talk to your parents about what you might want your teacher to know about OCD and what type of plan you can come up with. Write what you want your teacher to know about OCD:

Hi _____

_____

_____

_____

_____

_____

_____

_____

_____

_____

_____

More for You to Do

This is the chart that Courtney's team created to keep track of her success at resisting her compulsions at school each week:

Daily Goal	Mon	Tues	Wed	Thurs	Fri
Did you ask five or fewer questions?					

You earn **fifteen minutes of screen time** for every day you earn a star!

Here is an empty chart, which you and your team can use to track and reward you for resisting compulsions at school. Fill in your daily goal and the reward you will earn for meeting that goal. Ask your parents for help when completing this chart.

Daily Goal	Mon	Tues	Wed	Thurs	Fri

You earn _____ for every day you earn a star!

Now you know what to do if OCD follows you to school. By working with your caregivers and your teachers, you will become stronger than OCD!

Activity 26 Is OCD Hanging Out with You and Your Friends?

For You to Know

A lot of kids notice that OCD shows up when they are spending time with their friends, whether at school or just hanging out. OCD can interfere with friendships because it makes spending time with friends stressful or embarrassing. Unfortunately, this can lead you to avoid hanging out with other kids, but you don't have to let OCD take over your friendships. You can use stand-up statements and engage in brave challenges to become stronger than OCD.

Here is how Sam learned to stand up to OCD so that he could enjoy hanging out with his friends.

Sam noticed that OCD prevented him from spending time with his friends. Sam's OCD told him that he needed to wash his hands if he touched anything outside of his house. Sometimes he would have to wash his hands several times until OCD said his hands were clean. Sam had sticky thoughts that he would get very sick if he didn't follow these handwashing rules. When Sam would go to a friend's home to hang out, do homework, or play basketball, he would get so nervous about germs that he would try not to touch anything. If Sam did touch anything, he usually spent fifteen minutes in the bathroom washing his hands. When Sam's best friend, Paul, asked Sam about why he was in the bathroom so long, Sam didn't know what to say. Soon Sam stopped going to friends' homes or to parties for fear of getting sick. Sam realized that OCD was messing up his friendships, and he wanted to stand up to OCD. Sam's dad suggested that he come up with a plan to do brave challenges at his friends' homes and come up with stand-up statements to help him.

Does Sam's story sound familiar? Does OCD have rules for you to follow when you are with friends?

OCD Workbook for Kids

For You to Do

Sam and his dad decided to generate stand-up statements to use when OCD was making up silly rules. Here is a list of Sam's OCD rules and the stand-up statements that he came up with.

Sam's OCD Rules	Sam's Stand-Up Statements
You should stay home because you might get sick.	I'd rather risk getting sick than miss playing basketball!
There are lots of germs on that basketball.	I'll just notice my sticky thoughts and then pay attention to the game!
You need to wash your hands until they feel clean.	I am not going to follow your rules, OCD!

What rules does OCD want you to follow when you are with friends? What type of stand-up statements can you use? Write them in the space provided.

OCD's Rules	Your Stand-Up Statements

More for You to Do

Sam's dad helped him come up with a brave-challenge plan to become stronger than OCD. Below is the brave-challenge tower that Sam created with his dad.

Steve's Brave-Challenge Tower

Brave Challenge	Rating
Spend an hour playing basketball with Paul. Do not wash hands until after dinner.	9
Spend an hour playing basketball with Paul. Do not wash hands until it is time to eat dinner.	7
Spend an hour playing basketball with Paul. Do not wash hands until I come home.	6
Spend forty-five minutes playing basketball with Paul. Do not wash hands until I come home.	5
Spend thirty minutes playing basketball with Paul. Do not wash hands until I come home.	3

Sam was really nervous to do these brave challenges, but he knew he didn't want OCD messing up his friendships, so he gave it a try and slowly moved up the brave-challenge tower until OCD no longer messed up playing basketball with Paul. Sam was finally able to go to Paul's house and hang out for long periods of time without worrying about getting sick.

If you notice that OCD is getting in the way of your friendships, you may want to add brave challenges that involve your friends. With the help of a team member, think of brave challenges that you want to try and add these to your brave-challenge tower. Rate the brave challenges using your rating scale.

Don't forget to use all the skills you have learned as you make your way up the brave-challenge tower!

When You Don't Feel So Strong

For You to Know

Getting stronger than OCD is hard work, and there are times when you may not feel all that strong, or ready to do the brave challenges you need to do to stand up to OCD.

> Mariel was bothered a lot by her OCD but was just too busy to do brave challenges. After school, she usually had basketball or chorus, and then she needed to complete her homework. Her parents both worked and did not get home until six o'clock every night, so they weren't available to help her with brave challenges earlier in the day. When Mariel and her parents noticed that her OCD was getting a little worse, they worked to identify the problems getting in the way of Mariel doing brave challenges and saying no to compulsions.

If you are struggling with doing brave challenges, it's important to figure out what's getting in the way. Here are some things that may get in the way of working on your OCD, along with some ideas for how to solve these problems.

Not Feeling Motivated or Ready

You may feel like you would rather live with OCD than work on it. Or you may feel like your brave challenges are just too hard to face over and over, or that it will feel too scary to say no to compulsions. Here are some possible solutions:

Identify one part of OCD that you would like to face. You may not feel ready to take on all of your OCD, but are there one or two brave challenges that you are willing to try? Or are you willing to say no to just one compulsion? Taking on just part of OCD is a great start and may help you feel better!

Make a list of pros and cons. Ask a member of your OCD team to help you identify the pros of living with OCD (all the reasons why living with OCD is easier than standing up to OCD). Then identify the cons of living with OCD (the reasons why living with OCD is hard). Having more cons than pros on your list may mean it's worth working on OCD, even if it seems like a lot of hard work!

Not Having Enough Time to do Brave Challenges

You may feel that you cannot fit brave challenges into your life, because school and other activities take up so much time. Here are some possible solutions:

Schedule fifteen minutes every day as OCD practice time. Setting aside a specific time each day to work on OCD can help make it part of your daily routine. You can set an alarm or place a reminder on your refrigerator, so you don't forget!

Take a break from a daily activity while you are taking on OCD. Is there an activity or responsibility that you can take out of your daily schedule to help you fit in OCD practice time? You can work with your parents to help make time.

Not Having Enough Support

Perhaps your team may not always be available to help you as much as you need. Or perhaps OCD pops up at times when you are not around your team members. Here are some possible solutions:

Make a plan with your team. If there are certain times when OCD bothers you a lot, let your team know. This way, you can plan for a team member to be available at those times!

Add a team member. There may be places, like school, when your parents and other team members cannot help you so easily. If OCD bothers you at school, adding a trusted teacher or counselor to your team may help! If another adult besides your parents is with you often, that person may make a great team member too!

For You to Do

Are you having trouble completing brave challenges and saying no to compulsions? If so, try to identify what's getting in the way. Here's the list that Mariel and her parents made:

Problems That Make It Hard for Mariel to Work on OCD

I do not have enough time to work on OCD.

My team is not available to help me work on OCD.

If you're having trouble standing up to OCD, here's a list of problems that could be getting in your way. Circle the problems that make it hard to work on OCD. If you can identify different problems, add them to the list.

Problems that Make It Hard to Work on OCD

I don't want to work on my OCD right now.

I do not feel ready to work on my OCD right now.

I do not have enough time to work on OCD.

My team is not available to help me work on OCD.

_____

_____

_____

More for You to Do

Sit down with members of your team and review the problems that you circled. Come up with solutions to help solve these problems! As a guide, you can use the solutions listed earlier in this activity.

Here are the solutions that Mariel and her parents came up with:

1. **Leave chorus practice early once each week to make time for brave challenges.**

2. **Call Mom at work if OCD bothers me in the afternoon.**

3. **Add my babysitter to my team, so she can help me at home.**

What are your solutions to help you work on OCD? Discuss some good solutions with your team and write them down.

1. _____

2. _____

3. _____

4. _____

These strategies can help you complete brave challenges and say no to compulsions, even when you don't feel so strong. Do what you can each day to take on OCD!

Staying Strong!

For You to Know

Congratulations! If you have made it to the last activity of this book, you have probably worked hard on getting stronger than OCD! Hopefully you are noticing that OCD does not bother you so much anymore. This activity is about supporting all the great progress you have made. First read about Nancy, who also learned to better manage OCD.

> Nancy worked very hard to take control of OCD. She used to repeat herself four times when she spoke to make sure that others heard her perfectly, which took up *lots* of time. She also had to tap her fork and knife four times before picking them up at meals. It got so bad that Nancy sometimes avoiding talking to people or eating so that she would not have to repeat herself! After practicing brave challenges and saying no to compulsions, Nancy learned to resist repeating herself. It was very hard at first, but it got easier with time and practice. Nancy loved being able to say and do things only once!

Here are some things you should know about staying stronger than OCD:

OCD can come and go in waves. Sometimes it might bother you a lot, and sometimes just a little bit. OCD tends to bother kids a lot when there are changes in their lives, like starting a new school, a good friend moving away, or being chosen for the school play or a sports team. So it will be important to continue watching out for OCD clues to know when it starts to bother you more.

Continuing with brave challenges can help prevent OCD from getting strong again. After getting through this book, you may want to take a long break from doing brave challenges. That is understandable—you worked hard! But because OCD can sometimes come back and bother you more, it is important to keep practicing brave challenges. Just like you need to exercise regularly to keep your muscles strong, you need to keep doing brave challenges to keep you stronger than OCD! It can help to pick a specific time each day to practice a brave challenge, so it becomes part of your daily routine.

If a behavior feels even a little like a compulsion, say no to doing it! Part of staying stronger than OCD is making sure that new compulsions do not show up. As you know, OCD can be tricky—sometimes you can start doing a compulsion without even knowing it. If you notice yourself wanting to follow specific rules or routines during your day, it may be OCD trying to sneak back in. Remember, your job is to say no! It can be helpful to review the list of compulsions in activity 4 to remind yourself of different compulsions that can show up.

For You to Do

Keep track of your progress and your goals. To remember all her hard work and show her progress, Nancy made a list of goals that she had accomplished while working on OCD.

Nancy's Progress List

1. I can answer questions in class without repeating myself.

2. I can ask a question without repeating myself.

3. I can eat at the dinner table with my family.

4. I can pick up my fork and knife without tapping.

Nancy noticed that she still avoided eating at restaurants with her family because she first remembered doing compulsions at a restaurant. She also avoided talking to a few kids at school because in the past she got caught up in repeating herself when trying to talk with them. To keep track of situations that were still hard for her, Nancy made a second list of future goals.

Nancy's Future Goals

1. Eating at a restaurant with my family

2. Talking with Jessica and Kira at school

Make your own list of goals that you've accomplished and a second list of future goals! If you need help, ask a team member.

OCD Workbook for Kids

Your Progress List

1. _____
2. _____
3. _____
4. _____
5. _____
6. _____
7. _____

Your Future Goals

1. _____
2. _____
3. _____
4. _____
5. _____
6. _____
7. _____

Skills to Help Children Manage Obsessive Thoughts and Compulsive Behaviors

More for You to Do

The more you practice, the easier it will be to stay stronger than OCD! Use this worksheet to remember your skills and to keep track of all the great progress you continue to make.

Staying-Strong Worksheet

Which skills help you if OCD starts to bother you? Put a check mark by the ones that help.

☐ Rating my discomfort ☐ Doing brave challenges

☐ Talking to a team member ☐ Saying no to compulsions

☐ Using a stand-up statement ☐ Eating and sleeping right

☐ Just notice and be present ☐ Getting some exercise

Practice one brave challenge per day, even if it does not make you nervous anymore. Place a check mark in the box for every day you practice a brave challenge.

Month: _____

Sunday	Monday	Tuesday	Wednesday	Thursday	Friday	Saturday

What brave challenges are you especially proud of completing? Write them down:

_____

_____

Say no to all compulsions and look out for new compulsions! Write down the compulsions that you do not do as much anymore:

_____

You can use this worksheet every month or whenever you may need to remember. You can download copies at http://www.newharbinger.com/39782.

And, don't forget—this book is always here for you whenever you need help staying strong!

You are stronger than OCD! Keep up the great work!

A Caregiver's Guide to Brave Challenges

Do...	Don't...
Be honest with your child about what you are willing to do and what the brave challenge involves.	Lie to your child. ("I promise you that I washed my hands twice before I made your sandwich.")
Acknowledge to your child that brave challenges evoke anxiety.	Minimize the child's anxiety. ("It is so easy. There is nothing to be nervous about.")
Help your child break down daunting tasks into more manageable ones.	Let your child avoid situations that make her nervous.
Be flexible with the brave-challenge plan.	Tell your child that he must do every brave challenge as written.
Acknowledge to your child that there is always uncertainty and we must learn to face our fears.	Reassure or promise your child that everything will be okay and that nothing bad will happen if she does a brave challenge.
Help your child generate new brave-challenge ideas.	Tell your child that it is his job to do his OCD homework and that you are not responsible for helping.

Do...	Don't...
Positively reinforce your child with praise or rewards for completion of brave challenges. ("I saw how hard you worked on your OCD today," or "You earned your screen time for today because of doing your brave challenges.")	Pretend to not notice the reduction in compulsions for fear of calling too much attention to your child's OCD.
Encourage your child to complete an unplanned brave challenge when it occurs.	Tell your child she doesn't have to do an unplanned brave challenge if it was not discussed in advance.
Keep completing brave challenges until OCD is no longer present.	Take vacations from completing brave challenges because your child needs a break from working so hard on OCD.
Stay calm, even when your child is resistant to working on brave challenges.	Threaten your child with empty threats when struggling to complete brave challenges. ("You will be grounded for three months if you don't do your brave challenges.")

You can download a copy of this caregiver's guide at http://www.newharbinger.com/39782.

References

de Bruin, E. I., J. E. van der Zwan, and S. M. Bögels. 2016. "A RCT Comparing Daily Mindfulness Meditations, Biofeedback Exercises, and Daily Physical Exercise on Attention Control, Executive Functioning, Mindful Awareness, Self-Compassion, and Worrying in Stressed Young Adults." *Mindfulness* 7 (5): 1182–92.

Freeman, J., A. Garcia, H. Frank, K. Benito, C. Conelea, M. Walther, and J. Edmunds. 2014. "Evidence Base Update for Psychosocial Treatments for Pediatric Obsessive-Compulsive Disorder," *Journal of Clinical Child and Adolescent Psychology* 43 (1): 7–26.

Jones, M. C. 1924. "A Laboratory Study of Fear: The Case of Peter." *The Pedagogical Seminary and Journal of Genetic Psychology* 31: 308–15.

March, J. S., and K. Mulle. 1998. *OCD in Children and Adolescents: A Cognitive-Behavioral Treatment Manual.* New York: The Guilford Press.

POTS (Pediatric OCD Treatment Study Team). 2004. "Cognitive-Behavior Therapy, Sertraline, and Their Combination for Children and Adolescents with Obsessive-Compulsive Disorder: The Pediatric OCD Treatment Study (POTS) Randomized Controlled Trial." *Journal of the American Medical Association*, 292 (16), 1969–76.

Ruscio A. M., D. J. Stein, W. T. Chiu, and R. C. Kessler. 2010. "The Epidemiology of Obsessive-Compulsive Disorder in the National Comorbidity Survey Replication." *Molecular Psychiatry* 15 (1): 53–63.

Anthony C. Puliafico, PhD, is a clinical psychologist and director of the Columbia University Clinic for Anxiety and Related Disorders-Westchester. He is a renowned expert in the assessment and treatment of anxiety disorders and obsessive-compulsive disorder (OCD) in children, adolescents, and young adults.

Joanna A. Robin, PhD, is a clinical psychologist and director of Westchester Anxiety Treatment Psychological Services, P.C. She specializes in cognitive behavioral therapy (CBT), and is an expert in the treatment of anxiety, OCD, and behavioral problems.

Both Puliafico and Robin practice in Westchester, NY.

Foreword writer **Anne Marie Albano, PhD**, is professor of medical psychology in psychiatry at Columbia University, and director of the Columbia University Clinic for Anxiety and Related Disorders.

Register your **new harbinger** titles for additional benefits!

When you register your **new harbinger** title—purchased in any format, from any source—you get access to benefits like the following:

- Downloadable accessories like printable worksheets and extra content

- Instructional videos and audio files

- Information about updates, corrections, and new editions

Not every title has accessories, but we're adding new material all the time.

Access free accessories in 3 easy steps:

1. Sign in at NewHarbinger.com (or **register** to create an account).

2. Click on **register a book**. Search for your title and click the **register** button when it appears.

3. Click on the **book cover or title** to go to its details page. Click on **accessories** to view and access files.

That's all there is to it!

If you need help, visit:

NewHarbinger.com/accessories

new harbinger
CELEBRATING
40 YEARS

MORE BOOKS *from*
NEW HARBINGER PUBLICATIONS

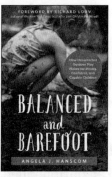